Workbook for GREGG Shorthand

Including Functional Method

Louis A. Leslie / Charles E. Zoubek

Shorthand written by Jerome P. Edelman

series 90

Gregg Division
McGraw-Hill Book Company
New York / St. Louis / Dallas / San Francisco / Auckland
Bogotá / Düsseldorf / Johannesburg / London / Madrid
Mexico / Montreal / New Delhi / Panama / Paris / São Paulo
Singapore / Sydney / Tokyo / Toronto

Workbook for Gregg Shorthand, Including Functional Method, Series 90

34567890 DODO 7865432109

ISBN 0-07-024473-1

Your workbook

The purpose of *Workbook for Gregg Shorthand, Series 90,* is to help you become a good stenographer who can take dictation rapidly and turn out mailable letters that are correctly punctuated and that contain no errors in spelling and grammar. In this workbook you will find drills that are especially designed to do the following things for you:

1 Develop your ability to build shorthand outlines for new words from outlines that you already know.

2 Develop your ability to construct shorthand outlines for words that are unfamiliar to you.

3 Increase your vocabulary.

4 Improve your ability to spell.

5 Improve your ability to punctuate.

6 Improve your mastery of English grammar.

If you practice the drills in this workbook faithfully, you will be delighted with the way your shorthand skill will grow and your ability to handle the mechanics of the English language will improve.

Practice suggestions

EVOLUTION DRILLS

In Part 1 you will devote most of your practice in each lesson to Evolution Drills. The purpose of these drills is to help you build shorthand outlines for new words from the shorthand outlines that you already know.

In the Evolution Drills you will be given the shorthand outline for the first item on each line. Using that outline as a guide, you are to fill in the shorthand outlines for the rest of the items on the line.

Examples

Words

In the workbook you will find:

see -s -ing *save* -s -ing

or

hope -s -ing -d

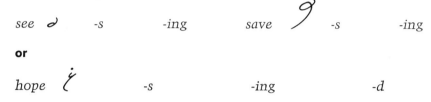

The completed drills will look like this:

see -s -ing *save* -s -ing

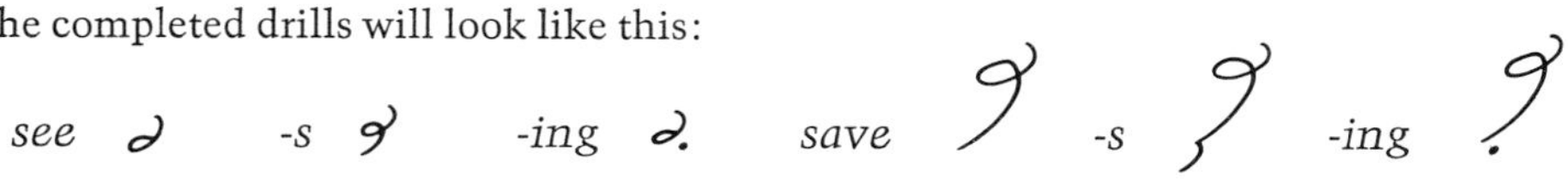

or

hope -s -ing -d

Word Beginnings

In the workbook you will find:

**overcoat* -stay -bid -come

*All the items on the line are to be based on the underscored syllable, word, or phrase.

The completed drill will look like this:

overcoat -stay -bid -come

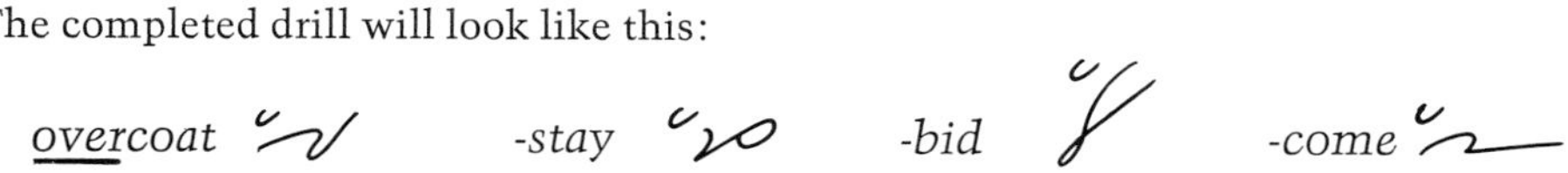

Word Endings

In the workbook you will find:

neatly great- nice- fair-

The completed drill will look like this:

neatly great- nice- fair-

Phrases

In the workbook you will find:

in the  *-that* *-this* *-our*

or

in the  *on-* *at-* *with-*

The completed drills will look like this:

in the  *-that*  *-this*  *-our* 

or

in the  *on-*  *at-*  *with-* 

Practice the Evolution Drills in this way:

1 Spell and read aloud the shorthand outline that introduces each drill; thus, *"s-e, see."* (Do not, however, spell brief forms and phrases; simply read them aloud without spelling.)

2 Write the shorthand outlines for the remaining items on the line, saying each word or phrase aloud as you write.

3 Whenever you meet a form for which you cannot immediately construct an outline, "make a stab at it" and proceed at once to the next outline.

4 The next day in class consult your teacher or your classmates about any outlines that gave you trouble.

OTHER DRILLS

Instructions for practicing the other types of drills in Part 1 are given at the point where the drills are first introduced.

TIME GOALS

Shorthand, to be of value, must be written and read rapidly. The quicker you can finish each lesson (always writing legible shorthand, of course!), the more benefit you will derive from it—and the sooner you will be through with your assignment.

Therefore, why not set a goal for the completion of each lesson in this workbook. Here are some time goals for you to shoot at in Part 1:

Lessons 1 through 6	12 minutes
Lessons 7 through 12	10 minutes
Lessons 13 through 18	9 minutes
Lessons 19 through 24	8 minutes
Lessons 25 through 30	7 minutes

You should be able to achieve these goals if you follow the practice suggestions that have been outlined for you.

PART 1

Lessons 1-30

NAME____ DATE______________

Lesson 1–2

OMISSION OF SILENT LETTERS

In Lesson 1 of your textbook you learned that silent letters are not written in shorthand. In the following words cross out the letters in each word that would not be written in shorthand because they are not pronounced.

snow	*aid*	*right*	*knee*	*steam*	*main*
day	*heat*	*say*	*slow*	*save*	*tow*

REPRESENTATION OF SOUNDS

Some sounds are represented in the English language in a number of ways. For example, the sound of *f* is also represented by *gh* and *ph*. In the following words indicate the sound represented by the underscored letter or letters.

cake k	*ceiling*	*dry*	*cough*	*Phil*	*quick*
graph	*saves*	*eight*	*neighbor*	*rough*	*ease*
race	*psychology*	*age*	*receive*	*easy*	*cat*

ALPHABET REVIEW

If you are to reach the point where you can write a shorthand outline for any word you hear, whether it is familiar to you or not, you must have a command of the shorthand alphabet. You must be able to recognize and write the strokes of Gregg Shorthand as rapidly as you can the letters of the longhand alphabet.

Under each of the following shorthand letters, write its longhand meaning.

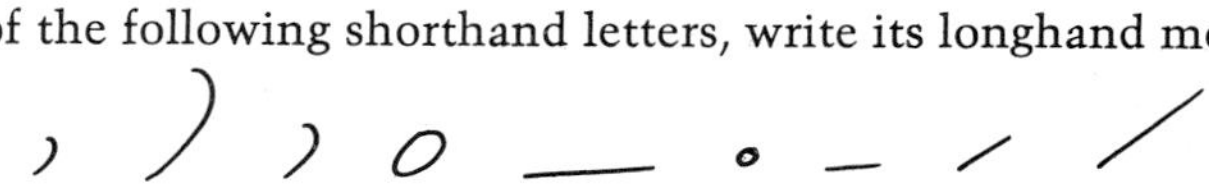

....

....

PUNCTUATION

Show how each of the following would be indicated in your shorthand notes.

period	*paragraph*	*dash*	*parentheses*
question mark	*hyphen*	*colon*	*semicolon*

EVOLUTION DRILLS

Before you begin your work on the following drills, read the practice suggestions on page 5.

1 *safe* -s   save -s   see -s

2 *hear* -ing   *heat* -ing   *phone* -ing

3 *try* -ing   *rate* -ing   *free* -ing

4 *read* -ing   own -ing   *need* -ing

5 *dry* -ing -d   write -ing -r

6 *sign* -ing -r   *deal* -ing -r

7 *fail* -ing   *feel* -ing

8 *line* -ing   *mail* -ing

9 *date* -ing   *stay* -ing

10 *light* -ing -r   *face* -ing

11 *leave* -ing   *mine* -ing

12 *lead* -ing   *strive* -ing

13 *zone* -ing   *flee* -ing

14 *know* -ing   snow -ing

15 *rely* -ing   *drive* -r

NAME________________________________ DATE______________

Lesson 3

ALPHABET REVIEW

Here are the shorthand strokes you studied in Lessons 1 through 3. Underneath each shorthand letter, write its longhand meaning.

....

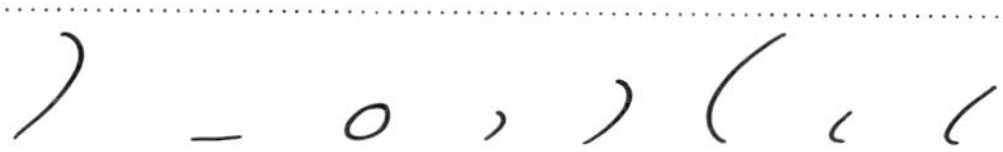

....

BRIEF FORMS

A number of brief forms have more than one meaning. In each of the following sentences a brief form that has more than one meaning is written in shorthand. In the space provided, transcribe the meaning that is correct.

	Correct Transcript
1 *He came to office.*	our
2 *I am feeling well.*	....
3 *I own car.*	....
4 *I think is late.*	....
5 *He leave soon.*	....
6 *These desks new.*	....
7 *He paid rent.*	....
8 *My train leaves in an .*	....
9 *John is not .*	....
10 *I will eat home.*	....

EVOLUTION DRILLS

Be sure to follow the instructions on page 5 of this workbook when you practice these drills.

1 *write*	*-s*	*-ing*	*-r*
2 *hope*	*-s*	*-ing*	*-d*
3 *type*	*-s*	*-ing*	*-d*
4 *sail*	*-s*	*-ing*	*-r*
5 *read*	*-ing*	*-s*	*-r*

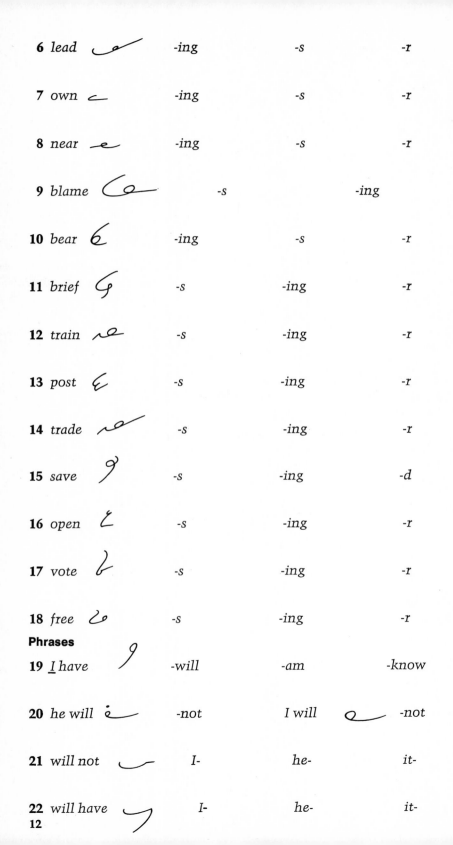

6	*lead* 	-ing	-s	-r
7	own 	-ing	-s	-r
8	*near* 	-ing	-s	-r
9	*blame* 	-s	-ing	
10	*bear* 	-ing	-s	-r
11	*brief* 	-s	-ing	-r
12	*train* 	-s	-ing	-r
13	*post* 	-s	-ing	-r
14	*trade* 	-s	-ing	-r
15	*save* 	-s	-ing	-d
16	*open* 	-s	-ing	-r
17	vote 	-s	-ing	-r
18	*free* 	-s	-ing	-r

Phrases

19	*I have* 	-will	-am		-know
20	*he will* 	-not	*I will*		-not
21	will not 	I-	he-		it-
22	will have 	I-	he-		it-

NAME____ DATE____________________

Lesson 4

ALPHABET REVIEW

Underneath each shorthand letter, write its longhand meaning.

....

....

....

EVOLUTION DRILLS

In the spaces provided, write the correct shorthand forms.

1 *move*  -s -ing -r

2 *renew*  -s -ing -al

3 *rule*  -s -ing -r

4 *wait*  -s -ing -r

5 *keep*  -s -ing -r

6 *make*  -s -ing -r

7 *grow*  -s -ing -r

8 *lose*  -ing -r -rs

9 *increase*  -d -ing

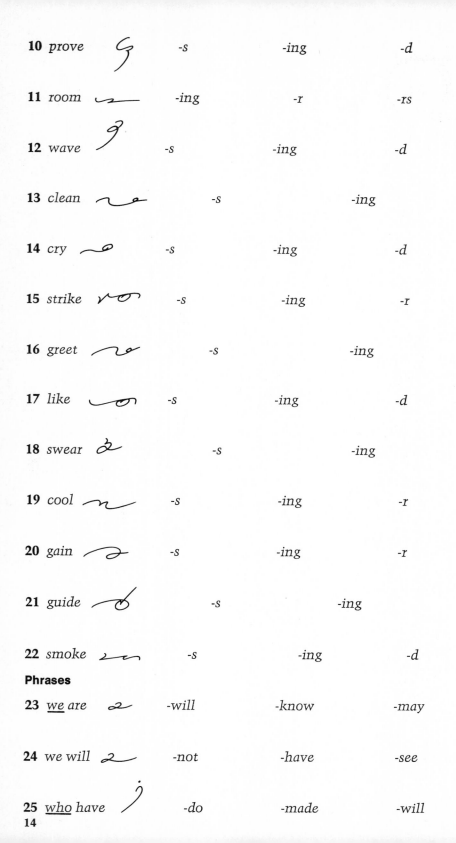

10 *prove*  *-s* *-ing* *-d*

11 *room*  *-ing* *-r* *-rs*

12 *wave*  *-s* *-ing* *-d*

13 *clean*  *-s* *-ing*

14 *cry*  *-s* *-ing* *-d*

15 *strike*  *-s* *-ing* *-r*

16 *greet*  *-s* *-ing*

17 *like*  *-s* *-ing* *-d*

18 *swear*  *-s* *-ing*

19 *cool*  *-s* *-ing* *-r*

20 *gain*  *-s* *-ing* *-r*

21 *guide*  *-s* *-ing*

22 *smoke*  *-s* *-ing* *-d*

Phrases

23 *we are*  *-will* *-know* *-may*

24 *we will*  *-not* *-have* *-see*

25 *who have*  *-do* *-made* *-will*

NAME____________________________________ DATE______________

Lesson 5

ALPHABET REVIEW

In Lessons 1 through 5 you have already studied more than half the strokes of Gregg Shorthand. See how well you remember those strokes by writing the longhand meaning underneath each shorthand stroke.

....

....

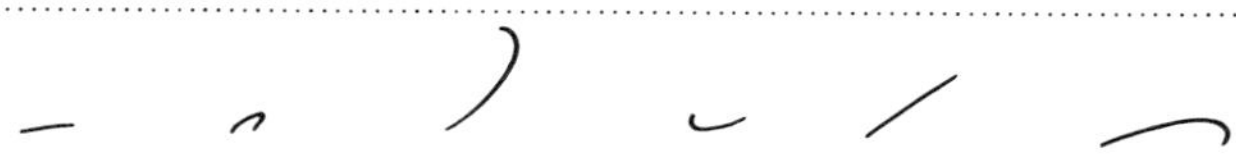

....

BRIEF FORMS

Transcribe the correct meaning of each brief form that is written in shorthand in the following sentences.

	Correct Transcript		Correct Transcript
1 *I received*  *check.*	....	**5** *He leaves*  *6 o'clock.*	....
2 *John*  *going home.*	....	**6** *Take*  *time.*	....
3 *Here is*  *share.*	....	**7** *John knows him*  *.*	....
4 *When will*  *arrive?*	....	**8** *James may* *run.*	....

EVOLUTION DRILLS

In the spaces provided, write the correct shorthand forms.

1 *act* 	*-s*	*-ing*	*-r*
2 *arrive* 	*-s*	*-ing*	*-d*
3 *farm* 	*-s*	*-ing*	*-r*
4 *start* 	*-s*	*-ing*	*-r*

5 *great*  *-r* *-est*

6 *sell*  *-s* *-ing* *-r*

7 *visit*  *-s* *-ing* *-r*

8 *serve*  *-s* *-ing* *-d*

9 *worry*  *-s* *-ing* *-d*

10 *throw*  *-s* *-ing* *-n*

11 *thick*  *-r* *-ness*

12 *bathe*  *-s* *-ing* *-d*

13 *health*  *-y* *wealth*  *-y*

14 *help*  *-s* *-r* *-d*

15 *win*  *-s* *-ing* *-r*

16 *live*  *-s* *-ing* *-d*

17 *radio*  *-s* *stereo*  *-s*

Phrases

18 *of our*  *-the* *-these* *-that*

19 *if the*  *in-* *at-* *to-*

20 *I can*  *you-* *we-* *who-*

21 *who will*  *-are* *-might* *-may*

NAME____________________ DATE____________

Lesson 6

RECALL

ALPHABET REVIEW

Underneath each shorthand letter write its longhand meaning. Can you do this in 45 seconds or less?

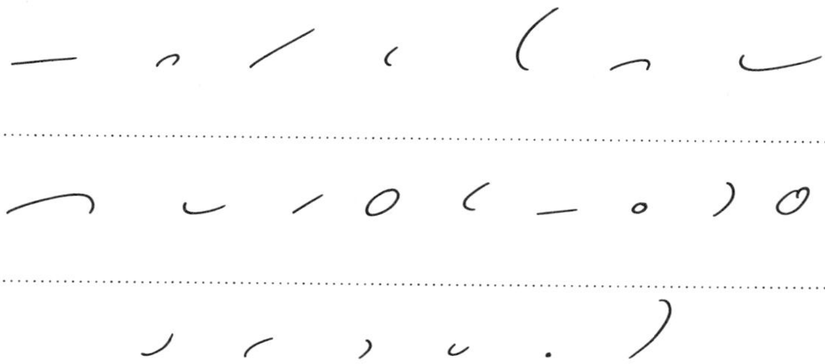

BRIEF FORMS

In the following sentences transcribe the underscored brief form.

		Correct Transcript			Correct Transcript
1		....	5	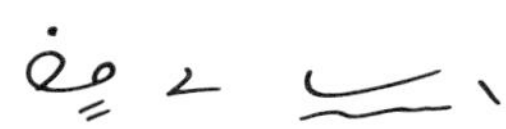	....
2		....	6		....
3		....	7	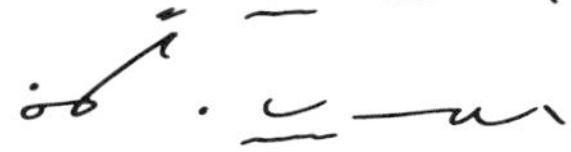	....
4		....	8	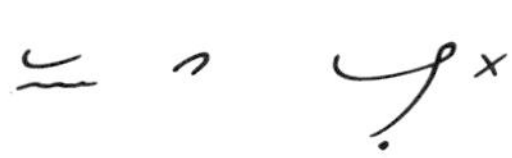	....

EVOLUTION DRILLS

In the spaces provided, write the correct shorthand forms.

1 *plan*  *-s* *-ing* *-r*

2 *relieve*  *-s* *-ing* *-d*

3 *own*  *-s* *-ing* *-r*

4 *travel*  *-s* *-ing* *-r*

5	*swim*		-s	-ing	-r
6	*wire*		-s	-ing	-less
7	*clean*		-s	-ing	-r
8	*care*		-s	-ing	-less
9	*take*		-s	-ing	-n
10	*give*		-s	-ing	-n
11	*thick*		-r		-ness
12	*agree*		-s	-ing	-d
13	*approve*		-s	-ing	-d
14	*wrap*		-s	-ing	-r
15	*harm*		-s	-ing	-less
16	*invest*		-s	-ing	-r
17	*throw*		-s	-ing	-n

Phrases

18	*we did*		-have	-made	-might
19	*with him*		-the	-that	-these
20	*I might*	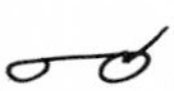	-can	-will	-may
21	*you do*		-will	-can	-might

NAME________________________________ DATE______________

Lesson 7

EVOLUTION DRILLS

In the spaces provided, write the correct shorthand forms.

1 *insure*  -s -ing -ance

2 *cash*  -s -ing -d

3 *ship*  -s -ing -d

4 *check*  -s -ing -d

5 *reach*  -s -ing -d

6 *switch*  -ing -s -d

7 *change*  -s -ing -d

8 *urge*  -s -ing -d

9 *job*  -s -r -rs

10 *drop*  -s -ing -d

11 *wash*  -s -ing -d

12 *talk*  -s -ing -d

13 *spot*  -s -ing -less

14 *thought*  -s -less

15 *block*  *-s* *-ing* *-d*

16 *solve*  *-s* *-ing* *-d*

17 *separate*  *-ing* *-s* *-r*

18 *follow*  *-s* *-ing* *-r*

19 *occur*  *-s* *-ing* *-ence*

20 *golf*  *-ing* *-r* *-rs*

Phrases

21 *on it*  *-that* *-the* *-our*

22 *to talk*  *-go* *-gain* *-it*

23 *you may*  *-might* *-can* *-will*

24 *he thought*  *-will* *-might* *-can*

BUSINESS VOCABULARY BUILDER

A large vocabulary is a great asset to the stenographer. The Business Vocabulary Builders in your textbook will help you develop your vocabulary. If you studied the Business Vocabulary Builder in Lesson 7, you can complete the following exercise quickly.

Write the underscored words in longhand; then define them briefly.

Example:

1 

vital Very important.

2 

3 

NAME ______________________________ DATE ______________

Lesson 8

BRIEF FORMS

In the following sentences transcribe the correct meaning of each brief form that is underscored.

	Correct Transcript		Correct Transcript
1 	....	4 	....
2 	....	5 	....
3 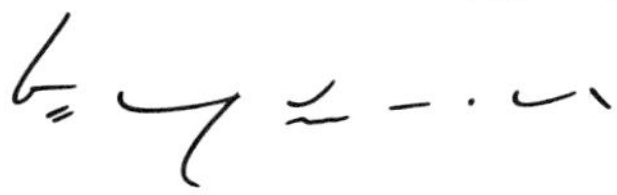	....	6 	....

EVOLUTION DRILLS

In the spaces provided, write the correct shorthand forms.

1 *begin*  *-s* *-ing* *-r*

2 *believe*  *-s* *-ing* *-r*

3 *brief*  *-s* *-r* *-ly*

4 *fair*  *-s* *-r* *-ly*

5 *cost*  *-s* *-ing* *-ly*

6 *light*  *-s* *-ing* *-ly*

7 *open*  *-s* *-ing* *-ly*

8 *name*  *-s* *-ing* *-ly*

9 *clean*  *-s* *-ing* *-ly*

10 *firm*  *-s* *-r* *-ly*

11 *clear*  *-ing* *-r* *-ly*

12 *like*  *-s* *-ing* *-ly*

13 *separate*  *-s* *-ing* *-ly*

14 *betray*  *-s* *-ing* *-d*

Phrases

15 *by it*  *-that* *-the* *-them*

16 *for me*  *-my* *-the* *-that*

17 *there will*  *-are* *-is* *-may*

18 *by this*  *in-* *at-* *on-*

19 *I would*  *he-* *you-* *who-*

20 *may be*  *would-* *might-* *will-*

BUSINESS VOCABULARY BUILDER

Write the underscored words in longhand; then define them briefly.

1 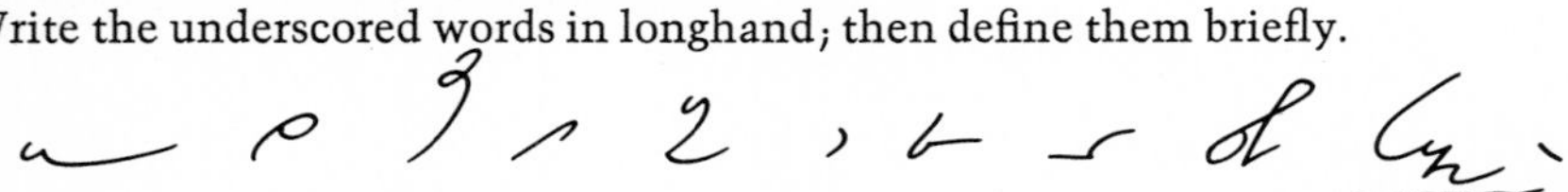

....

2 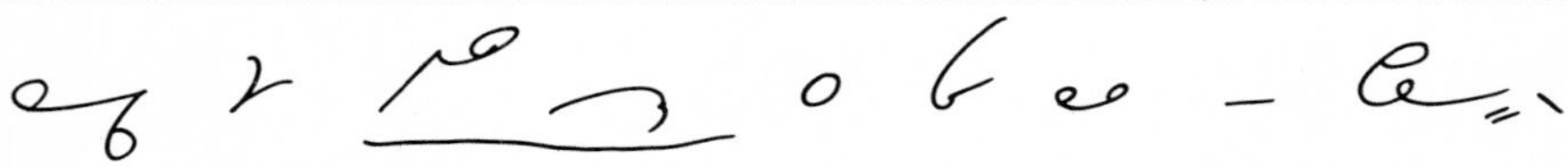

....

3 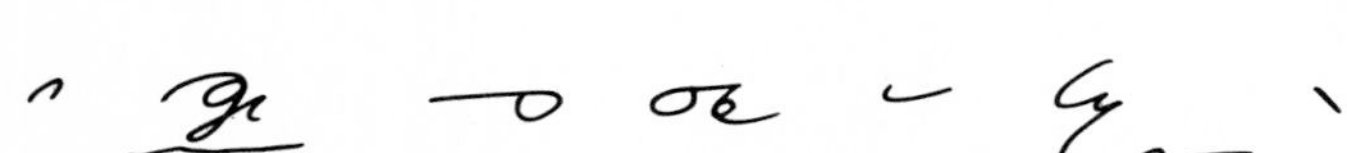

....

....

4 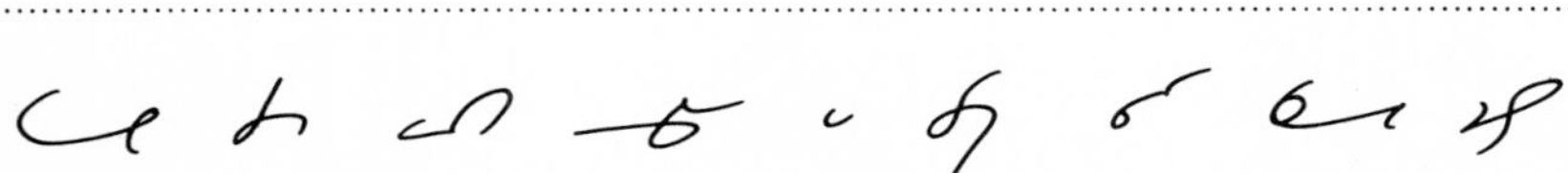

....

NAME ______________________________ DATE ______________

Lesson 9

EVOLUTION DRILLS

In the spaces provided, write the correct shorthand forms.

1 *motion* 	-s	-ing	-ed	
2 *occasion* 	-s	-al	-ally	
3 *option* 	-s	-al		
4 *nation* 	-s	-al	-ally	
5 *cancel* 	-s	-ing	-ation	
6 *operation* 	-s	-al		
7 *section* 	-s	-al		
8 *ration* 	-s	-ed	-al	
9 *patient* 	-s	-ly		
10 *efficient* 	-ly	*proficient* 	-ly	
11 *provision* 	-s	-al	-ally	
12 *prepare* 	-s	-ing	-ations	
13 *profession* 	-s	-al		
14 *promotion* 	-s	-al		

Phrases

15 to be  -have -put -which

16 to see  -say -sell -sail

17 to change  -check -charge -choose

18 to place  -prove -please -plan

Recall

19 *believe*  -s -ing -d

20 *begin*  -s -ing -r

21 *neatly*  *near-* *dear-* *nice-*

22 *needless*  *thought-* *fear-* *harm-*

23 *earnest*  *fin-* *near-* *late-*

24 *later*  *lead-* *read-* *farm-*

BUSINESS VOCABULARY BUILDER

Write the underscored word in longhand; then define it briefly.

1 

2 

3 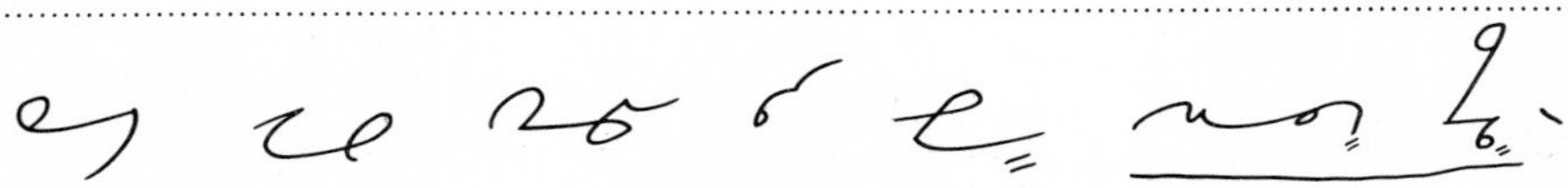

NAME ____________________ DATE ____________

Lesson 10

EVOLUTION DRILLS

In the spaces provided, write the correct shorthand forms.

1	*kind*		-*s*	-*ly*	-*r*
2	*rent*		-*s*	-*ing*	-*al*
3	*endorse*		-*ing*	-*d*	-*s*
4	*paint*		-*ing*	-*ed*	-*r*
5	*land*		-*ing*	-*s*	-*ed*
6	*earn*		-*s*	-*ing*	-*ed*
7	*prevent*		-*s*	-*ing*	-*ed*
8	*plan*		-*ing*	-*s*	-*ed*
9	*address*		-*ing*	-*ed*	-*es*
10	*please*		-*ing*	-*d*	-*s*
11	*close*		-*ing*	-*ly*	-*s*
12	*process*		-*ing*	-*ed*	-*es*
13	*place*		-*d*	-*ing*	-*s*
14	*notice*		-*ing*	-*d*	-*s*

15 *lease*  -*d* -*ing* -*s*

16 *release*  -*d* -*ing* -*s*

17 *trace*  -*s* -*ing* -*d*

Phrase Review

18 *in these*  -*the* -*that* -*this*

19 on it  -the -that -them

20 for this  -the -that -my

21 there is  -will -are -may

22 by which  -the -that -them

23 to put  -be -have -place

24 I might 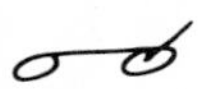 -will -can -would

25 he might 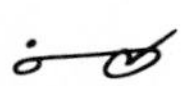 -may -will -can

BUSINESS VOCABULARY BUILDER

Transcribe the underscored words in longhand; then define them briefly.

1 

2

3 

NAME ______________________________ DATE ______________

Lesson 11

EVOLUTION DRILLS

In the spaces provided, write the correct shorthand forms.

1	*answer* 	-s	-ing	-ed
2	*offer* 	-s	-ing	-ed
3	*hire* 	-s	-ing	-d
4	*occur* 	-s	-ing	-ed
5	*retire* 	-s	-ing	-d
6	*favor* 	-s	-ing	-ed
7	*render* 	-s	-ing	-ed
8	*build* 	-ing	-s	-r
9	*fail* 	-s	-ing	-ed
10	*call* 	-s	-r	-ed
11	*fold* 	-s	-ing	-r
12	*hold* 	-s	-ing	-r
13	*seal* 	-s	-ing	-ed
14	*file* 	-s	-ing	-d

Phrases

15 *have been*  *you-* *I-* *who-*

16 *have not been*  *you-* *I-* *who-*

17 *have not been able*  *you-* *I-* *who-*

18 *should be able*  *you-* *I-* *he-*

19 *will be able*  *I-* *you-* *he-*

20 *would be able*  *I-* *he-* *you-*

21 *could be*  *I-* *he-* *you-*

22 *from these*  *-our* *-this* *-them*

23 *send you*  *-the* *-this* *-them*

24 *should be*  *I-* *you-* *who-*

25 *after them*  *-the* *-that* *-this*

BUSINESS VOCABULARY BUILDER

Write the underscored words in longhand; then transcribe them briefly.

1 

2 

3 

4 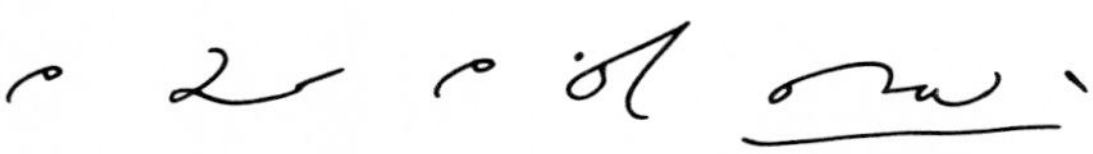

NAME ______________________________ DATE ______________

Lesson 12

RECALL

BRIEF FORMS

In the space provided, write the correct meaning of each underscored brief form.

	Correct Transcript		Correct Transcript
1 	....	5 	....
2 	....	6 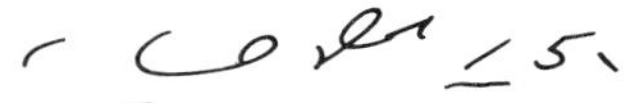	....
3 	....	7 	....
4 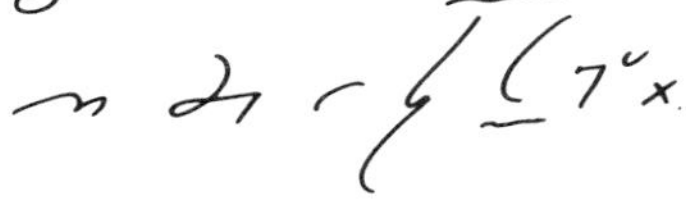	....	8 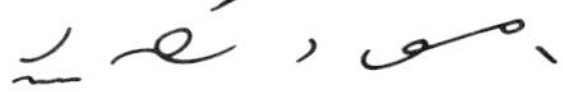	....

EVOLUTION DRILLS

In the spaces provided, write the correct shorthand forms.

1 *call* 	*-s*	*-ing*	*-ed*
2 *cost* 	*-s*	*-ing*	*-ly*
3 *clear* 	*-s*	*-r*	*-ly*
4 *wash* 	*-s*	*-ing*	*-ed*
5 *proficient* 	*-ly*	*efficient* 	*-ly*
6 *paint* 	*-s*	*-ing*	*-r*
7 *indicate* 	*-s*	*-ing*	*-r*
8 *bill* 	*-s*	*-ing*	*-ed*
9 *pass* 	*-ed*	*-ing*	*-es*
10 *trace* 	*-ing*	*-d*	*-s*

11 *wire*  -*s* -*ing* -*d*

12 *became*  -*cause* -*neath* -*tray*

13 *office*  -*r* -*rs* -*s*

14 *race*  -*d* -*ing* -*s*

Phrases

15 *to pay*  -*buy* -*show* -*plan*

16 *into these*  -*the* -*that* -*this*

17 *will be able*  *I*- *you*- *he*-

18 *have been able*  *I*- *you*- *who*-

19 *could be*  *I*- *you*- *he*-

20 *from him*  -*the* -*this* -*that*

21 *should be*  *who*- *you*- *he*-

22 *on them*  *to*- *with*- *of*-

BUSINESS VOCABULARY BUILDER

Write the underscored words in longhand; then define them briefly.

1 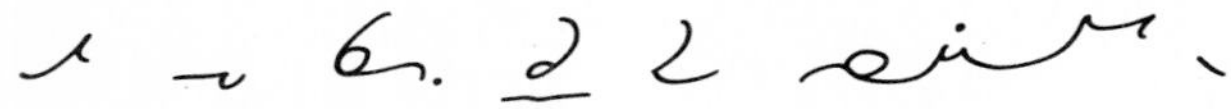

....

2 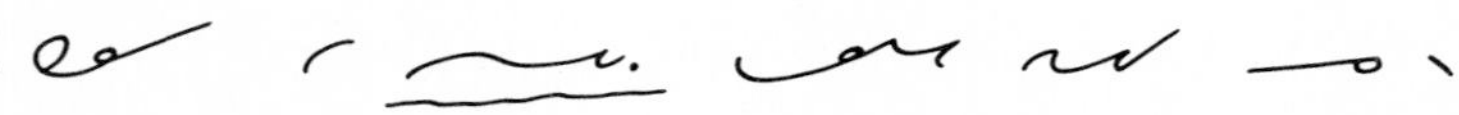

....

3 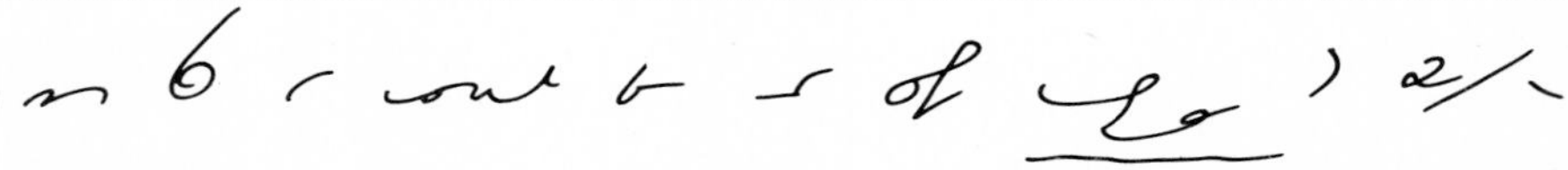

....

NAME______________________________ DATE______________

Lesson 13

EVOLUTION DRILLS

In the spaces provided, write the correct shorthand forms.

Brief Forms

1 *glad*  *-ly* *-ness*

2 *work*  *-s* *-ing* *-ed*

3 *order*  *-s* *-ing* *-ly*

4 *enclose*  *-s* *-ing* *-d*

5 *soon*  *-r* *circular*  *-s*

Phrases

6 *I enclosed*  *he-* *you-* *we-*

7 *be glad*  *I will-* *he will-* *you will-*

8 *I was*  *he-* *it-* *there-*

9 *thank you*  *-for* *-for the* *-for your*

10 *I must*  *you-* *he-* *we-*

Words

11 *cover*  *-s* *-ing* *-ed*

12 *color*  *-s* *-ing* *-ed*

13 *pull*  *-s* *-ing* *-ed*

14 *book*  *-s* *-ed* *-ing*

15 *number*  -s -ing -ed

16 *adjust*  -ing -s -r

17 *drug*  -s -ed -ist

18 *look*  -s -ing -ed

19 *dust*  -s -ing -r

20 *suffer*  -s -ing -ed

21 *cook*  -s -ing -ed

22 *hunt*  -s -ing -r

23 *utter*  -s -ing -ed

24 *illustrate*  -s -ing -r

BUSINESS VOCABULARY BUILDER

Write the underscored words in longhand; then define them briefly.

1 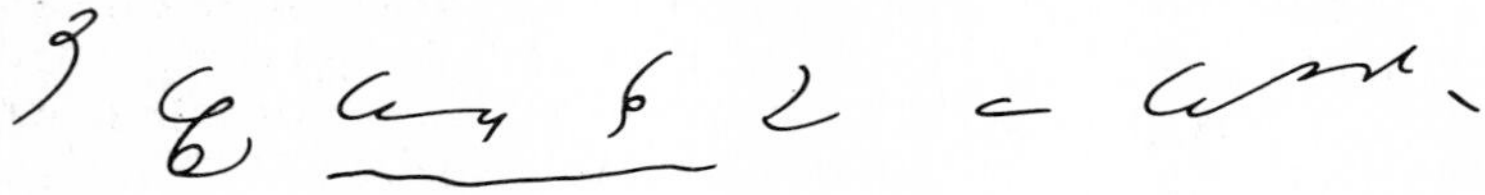

....

2 

....

3 

....

NAME____DATE____________________

Lesson 14

EVOLUTION DRILLS

In the spaces provided, write the correct shorthand forms.

1 *quick*		*-r*	*-ly*	*-ness*
2 *quote*		*-s*	*-ing*	*-d*
3 *list*		*-s*	*-ing*	*-ed*
4 *accept*		*-s*	*-ing*	*-ed*
5 *guide*		*-s*	*-ing*	*-d*
6 *deduct*		*-s*	*-ing*	*-ed*
7 *detail*		*-s*	*-ing*	*-ed*
8 *credit*		*-s*	*-r*	*-ed*
9 *edit*		*-s*	*-ing*	*-r*
10 *square*		*-s*	*-ly*	*-d*
11 *equip*		*-s*	*-ing*	*-ed*
12 *need*		*-s*	*-less*	*-ed*
13 *grade*		*-s*	*-ing*	*-d*
14 *dwell*		*-s*	*-ing*	*-ed*

15 *assert*  -s -ing -ed

16 *adopt*  -s -ing -ed

17 *study*  -s -ing -d

18 *wait*  -s -r -ed

19 *waste*  -s -ing -d

20 *audit*  -s -ing -r

21 *provide*  -s -ing -d

22 *railway*  Broad- road- path-

23 *treat*  -s -ing -ed

24 *invite*  -s -ing -d

BUSINESS VOCABULARY BUILDER

Write the underscored words in longhand; then define them briefly.

1 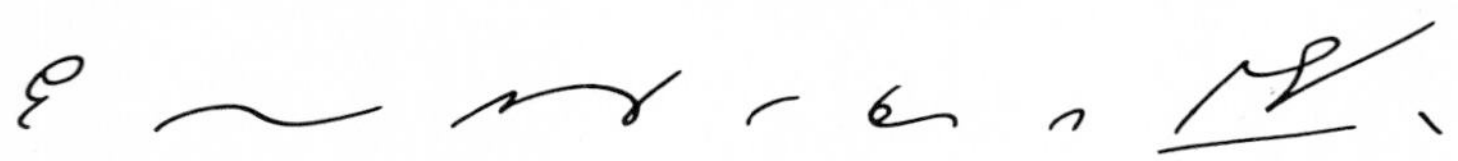

2 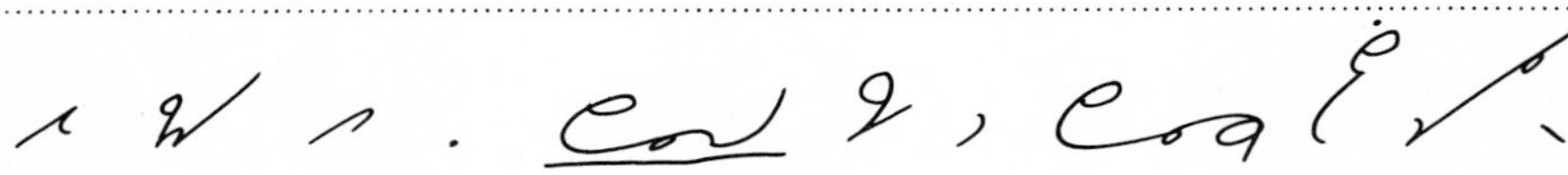

3 

NAME____ DATE____________________

Lesson 15

EVOLUTION DRILLS

In the spaces provided, write the correct shorthand forms.

Brief Forms

1 *value*  *-s* *-ble* *-less*

2 *think*  *-s* *-ing*

3 *business*  *-s* *-man* *-like*

4 *any* *-thing* *-one* *-body*

Phrases

5 *about it*  *-that* *-the* *-this*

6 *they think*  *I-* *you-* *we-*

7 *what will*  *-are* *-is* *-has*

8 *which one*  *this-* *for-* *each-*

Words

9 *accept*  *-s* *-ed* *-ble*

10 *avail*  *-s* *-ed* *-ble*

11 *honor*  *-s* *-ed* *-ble*

12 *reason*  *-s* *-ing* *-ble*

13 *revise*  *-s* *-d* *-ing*

14 *agree* 	-s	-ing	-ble
15 *favor* 	-s	-ed	-ble
16 *receive* 	-s	-ing	-d
17 *refer* 	-s	-ed	-ence
18 *repeat* 	-s	-ing	-ed
19 *resist* 	-s	-ing	-ed
20 *reply* 	-s	-d	-ing
21 *repair* 	-s	-ing	-ed
22 *rely* 	-s	-ing	-ble
23 *adjust* 	-r	-ed	-ble
24 *deduct* 	-s	-ed	-ble
25 *reprint*	-s	-ing	-ed

BUSINESS VOCABULARY BUILDER

Write the underscored words in longhand; then define them briefly.

1 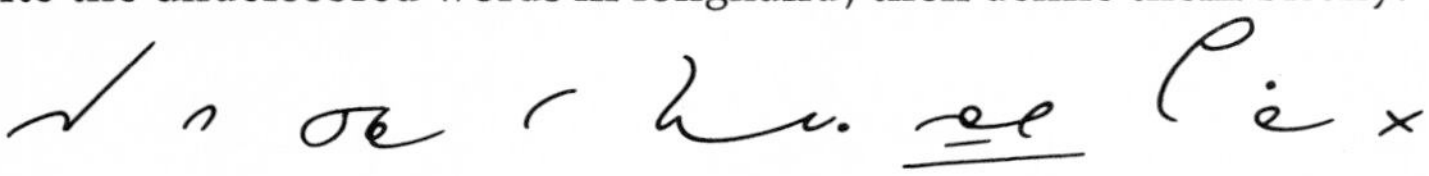

....

2 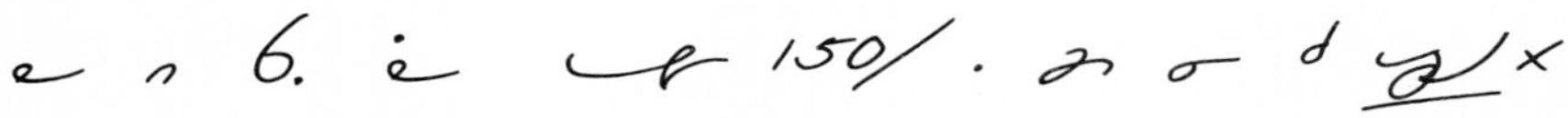

....

3 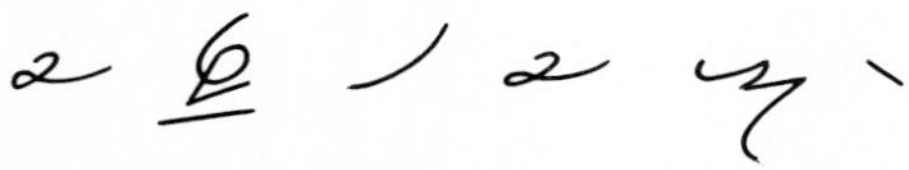

....

NAME____ DATE____________________

Lesson 16

EVOLUTION DRILLS

In the spaces provided, write the correct shorthand forms.

1 *annoy*  *-s* *-ing* *-ance*

2 *point*  *-s* *-ed* *-ing*

3 *appoint*  *-s* *-ing* *-ed*

4 *toil*  *-s* *-ing* *-ed*

5 *manage*  *-s* *-ing* *-d*

6 *fresh*  *-ly* *-ness* *-men*

7 *mention*  *-s* *-ing* *-ed*

8 *sale*  *-s* *-sman* *-smen*

9 *eliminate*  *-s* *-d*

10 *month*  *-s* *-ly*

11 *meant*  *-al* *-ally*

12 *join*  *-s* *-ing* *-ed*

13 *voice*  *-s* *-d* *-ing*

14 *yield* *-s* *-ing* *-ed*

15 *year* -s -ly

16 *yard* -s *yarn* -s

17 *yell* -s -ing -ed

Review

18 *cable* -s -ing -d

19 *pay* -s -ing -ble

20 *recheck* -s -ing -ed

21 *resign* -s -ing -ed

22 *suit* -s -ed -ble

23 *replace* -ing -d -s

Phrases

24 *<u>to</u> boil* -join -point -spoil

25 *<u>this</u> minute* -month -may -day

BUSINESS VOCABULARY BUILDER

Write the underscored words in longhand; then define them briefly.

1 

2 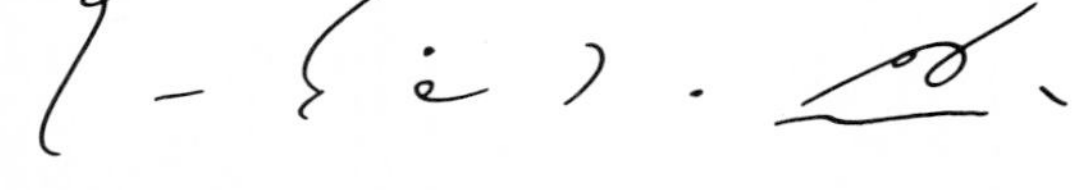

3 

NAME________________________________ DATE________________

Lesson 17

EVOLUTION DRILLS

In the spaces provided, write the correct shorthand forms.

Brief Forms and Phrases

1 *manufacture*  *-s* *-r* *-d*

2 *short*  *-r* *-ly* *-age*

3 *to persuade*  *-permit* *-purchase* *-plan*

4 *next day*  *-month* *-year* *-morning*

Words

5 *purchase*  *-ing* *-d* *-r*

6 *person*  *-s* *-al* *-ally*

7 *decide*  *-s* *-ing* *-d*

8 *deposit*  *-s* *-ing* *-r*

9 *direct*  *-s* *-r* *-ed*

10 *permit*  *-s* *-ing* *-ed*

11 *purpose*  *-s* *-ly*

12 *pursue*  *-d* *-ing* *-s*

13 *depend*  *-s* *-ent* *-ble*

14 *desire*  *-s* *-d* *-ble*

15 *delay*  -s -ing -d

16 *design*  -s -ing -r

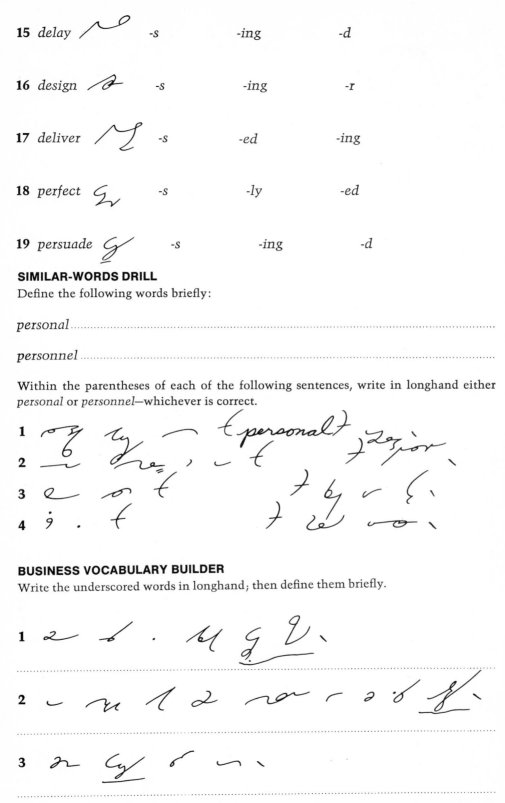

17 *deliver*  -s -ed -ing

18 *perfect*  -s -ly -ed

19 *persuade*  -s -ing -d

SIMILAR-WORDS DRILL

Define the following words briefly:

personal ....

personnel ....

Within the parentheses of each of the following sentences, write in longhand either *personal* or *personnel*—whichever is correct.

1
2
3
4

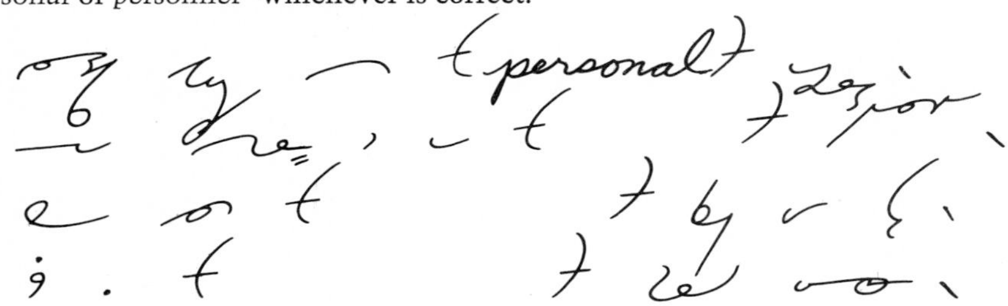

BUSINESS VOCABULARY BUILDER

Write the underscored words in longhand; then define them briefly.

1 

....

2 

....

3 

....

NAME____ DATE____________________

Lesson 18

RECALL

EVOLUTION DRILLS

In the spaces provided, write the correct shorthand forms.

Brief Forms

1 *work* *-ing* *-s* *-ed*

2 *order*  *-s* *-ing* *-ly*

3 *enclose*  *-s* *-ing* *-d*

4 *business*  *-s* *-men* *-like*

5 *manufacture*  *-ing* *-r* *-rs*

6 *short*  *-ly* *-r* *-age*

7 *value*  *-s* *-ble*

8 *any* *-thing* *-body* *-one*

Phrases

9 *I was*  *what-* *he-* *it-*

10 *thank you*  *-for* *-for the* *-for your*

11 *about this*  *-the* *-them* *-that*

12 *next month*   *-year* *-day* *-morning*

13 *to purchase*  *-put* *-push* *-join*

Words

14 *drug* -s -ed -ist

15 *pull* -s -ing -ed

16 *quote* -s -ing -d

17 *act* -s -r -ed

18 *favor* -s -ed -ble

19 *replace* -s -ing -d

20 *appoint* -s -ing -ed

21 *manage* -d -ing -s

22 *yell* -s -ing -ed

23 *direct* -s -ing -ed

24 *permit* -s -ing -ed

BUSINESS VOCABULARY BUILDER

Write the underscored words in longhand; then define them briefly.

1 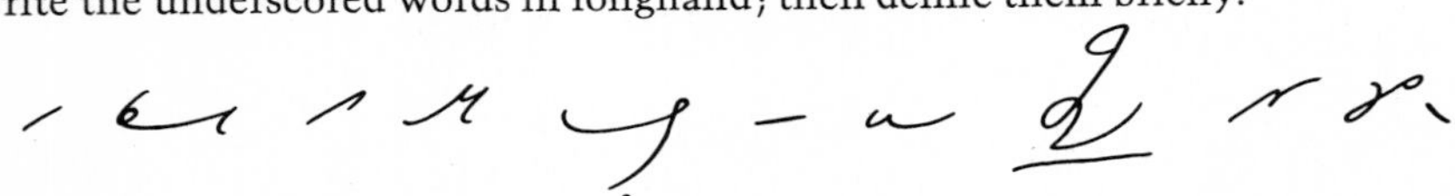

2 

3 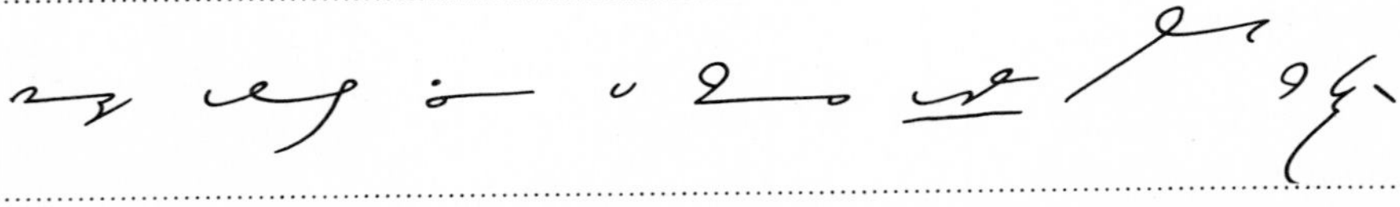

NAME______________________________ DATE______________

Lesson 19

EVOLUTION DRILLS

In the spaces provided, write the correct shorthand forms.

Brief Forms

1 *present*  *-ing* *-s* *-ed*

2 *advertise*  *-ing* *-s* *-ment*

3 *opportunity*  *-s* *immediate*  *-ly*

4 *part*  *-s* *-ly* *-ed*

5 *depart*  *-s* *-ing* *-ment*

Words

6 *use*  *-s* *-ing* *-d*

7 *review*  *-s* *-ing* *-ed*

8 *unite*  *-s* *-ing* *-d*

9 *arrange*  *-s* *-ing* *-ment*

10 *manage*  *-s* *-ing* *-ment*

11 *assign*  *-s* *-ing* *-ment*

12 *initial*  *-s* *-ing* *-ed*

13 *special*  *-ly* *financial*  *-ly*

14 *refuse*  *-d* *-ing* *-al*

15 *equip* -ed -s -ment

16 *invest* -s -ed -ment

17 *settle* -s -d -ment

18 *argue* -s -ing -ment

19 *accuse* -ing -d -s

20 *ship* -s -r -ment

21 *move* -s -d -ment

SPELLING REVIEW

Transcribe the following words in longhand being careful to spell them correctly. All of them appear in the margins of the Reading and Writing Practice of your book.

1 .... 5 ....

2 .... 6 ....

3 .... 7 ....

4 .... 8 ....

BUSINESS VOCABULARY BUILDER

Write the underscored words in longhand; then define them briefly.

1 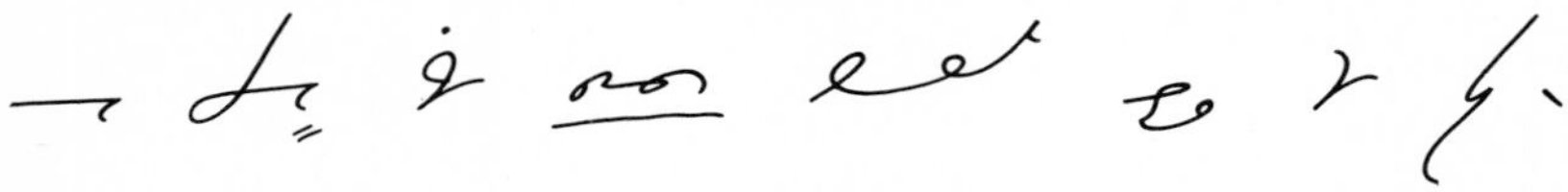

....

2 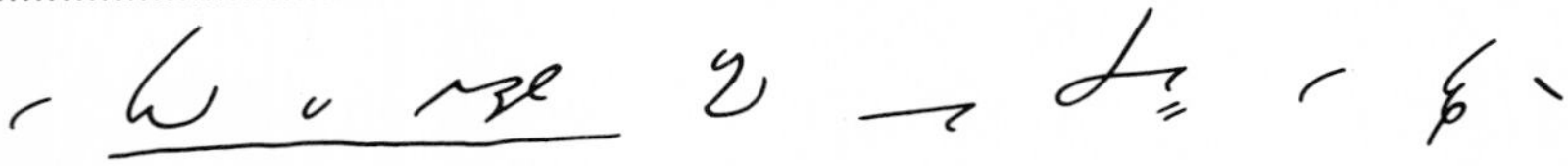

....

3 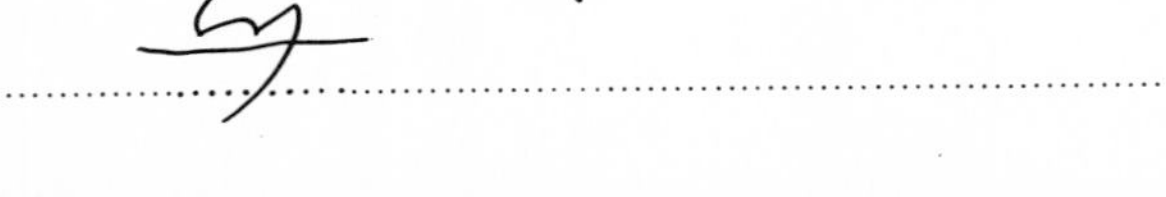

....

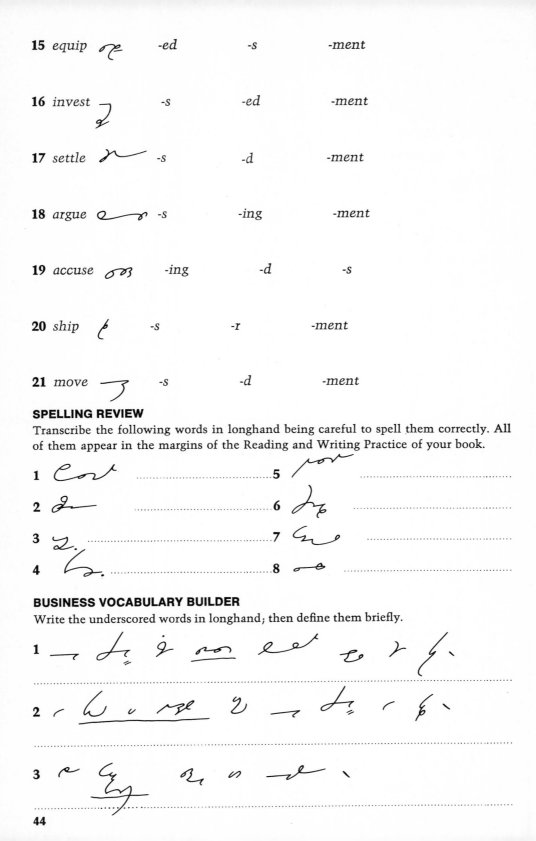

NAME____________________ DATE__________

Lesson 20

EVOLUTION DRILLS

In the spaces provided, write the correct shorthand forms.

1 *announce* 	*-ing*	*-d*	*-ment*
2 *account* 	*-s*	*-ing*	*-ed*
3 *crowd* 	*-s*	*-ing*	*-ed*
4 *loud* 	*-ly*	*-r*	*-est*
5 *gather* 	*-ing*	*-ed*	*-s*
6 *bother* 	*-s*	*-ing*	*-ed*
7 *consist* 	*-s*	*-ing*	*-ed*
8 *consider* 	*-s*	*-ed*	*-ble*
9 *concern* 	*-s*	*-ing*	*-ed*
10 *complete* 	*-s*	*-ing*	*-d*
11 *compliment* 	*-s*	*-ing*	*-ary*
12 *compute* 	*-s*	*-d*	*-r*
13 *house* 	*-ing*	*-s*	*-d*
14 *consign* 	*-s*	*-ing*	*-ment*

15 *allow* -s -ing -ance

16 *sound* -ed -r -ness

17 *consume* -s -r -rs

18 *control* -s -ing -ed

19 *compare* -s -ing -d

20 *complain* -s -ing -ed

21 *conclude* -s -ing -d

22 *confer* -s -ed -ence

SPELLING REVIEW

Transcribe the following words in longhand. Be sure to spell them correctly.

1 .... 5 ....

2 .... 6 ....

3 .... 7 ....

4 .... 8 ....

BUSINESS VOCABULARY BUILDER

Write the underscored words in longhand; then define them briefly.

1 

....

2 

....

3 

....

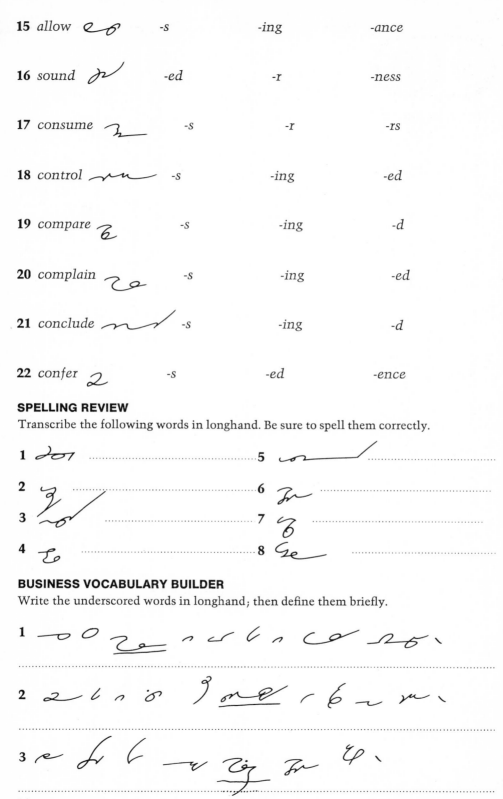

NAME ______________________ DATE ____________

Lesson 21

EVOLUTION DRILLS

In the spaces provided, write the correct shorthand forms.

Brief Forms and Phrases

1	*advantage* 	*-s*	*-ous*	*-ously*
2	*out* 	*-line*	*-side*	*-fit*
3	*every* 	*-one*	*-thing*	*-body*
4	*ever* 	*what-*	*where-*	*when-*
5	*every minute* 	*-month*	*-day*	*-other*
6	*several days* 	*-months*	*-minutes*	*-others*

Words

7	*deny* 	*-s*	*-ing*	*-d*
8	*danger* 	*-s*	*-ous*	*-ously*
9	*obtain* 	*-s*	*-ing*	*-ble*
10	*contain* 	*-s*	*-ing*	*-r*
11	*remit* 	*-s*	*-ing*	*-ance*
12	*attend* 	*-s*	*-ing*	*-ed*
13	*evident* 	*-ly*	*confident* 	*-ly*
14	*accident* 	*-s*	*-al*	*-ally*
15	*guide* 	*-s*	*-d*	*-ance*

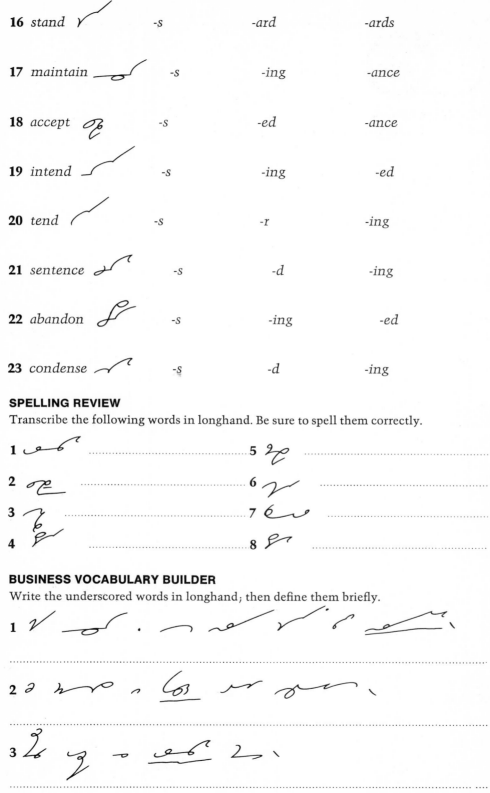

16 *stand*  *-s* *-ard* *-ards*

17 *maintain*  *-s* *-ing* *-ance*

18 *accept*  *-s* *-ed* *-ance*

19 *intend*  *-s* *-ing* *-ed*

20 *tend*  *-s* *-r* *-ing*

21 *sentence*  *-s* *-d* *-ing*

22 *abandon*  *-s* *-ing* *-ed*

23 *condense*  *-s* *-d* *-ing*

SPELLING REVIEW

Transcribe the following words in longhand. Be sure to spell them correctly.

1  .... 5  ....

2  .... 6  ....

3  .... 7  ....

4  .... 8  ....

BUSINESS VOCABULARY BUILDER

Write the underscored words in longhand; then define them briefly.

1 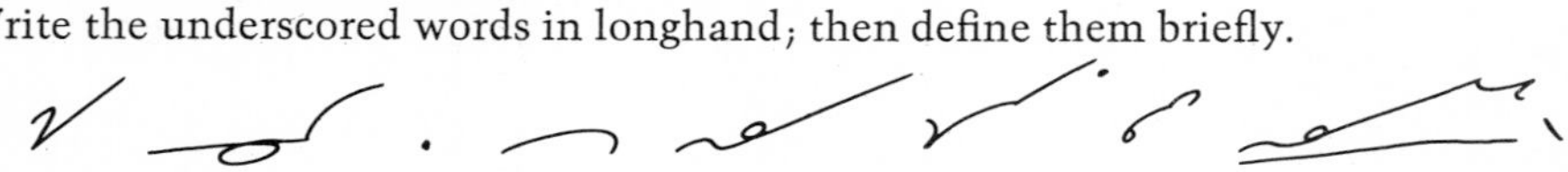

....

2 

....

3 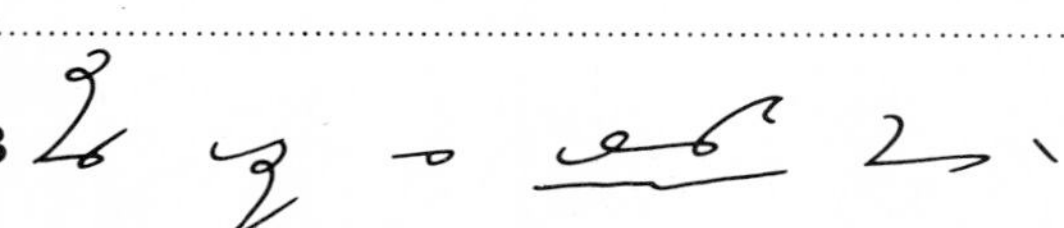

....

NAME________________________________ DATE________________

Lesson 22

EVOLUTION DRILLS

In the spaces provided, write the correct shorthand forms.

1 *damage*  *-s* *-ing* *-d*

2 *attempt*  *-s* *-ing* *-ed*

3 *estimate*  *-s* *-ing* *-d*

4 *custom*  *-s* *-r* *-rs*

5 *temper*  *-s* *-ed* *-ary*

6 *contemplate*  *-s* *-ing* *-d*

7 *sel<u>dom</u>*  *free-* *ran-*

8 *item*  *-s* *-ize* *-izing*

9 *bottom*  *-s* *-less*

10 *demonstrate*  *-s* *-ing* *-r*

11 *demand*  *-s* *-ing* *-ed*

Phrases

12 *<u>Dear</u> Mr.*  *-Mrs.* *-Miss* *-Ms.*

13 *<u>My dear</u> Mrs.*  *-Mr.* *-Miss* *-Ms.*

14 *<u>to</u> know*  *-make* *-me*

Days and Months

15 *Sunday*  *Monday* *Tuesday* *Friday*

16 *January*  *August* *December* *October*

17 *Friday morning*  *Tuesday-* *Thursday-*

Recall

18 *gather*  *-s* *-ing* *-ed*

19 *conceal*  *-s* *-ing* *-ed*

20 *compliment*  *-s* *-ing* *-ary*

21 *detain*  *-s* *-ing* *-ed*

22 *round*  *-s* *-ly* *-ness*

SPELLING REVIEW

Transcribe the following words in longhand. Watch your spelling!

1  .... 5  ....

2  .... 6  ....

3  .... 7  ....

4  .... 8  ....

BUSINESS VOCABULARY BUILDER

Write the underscored words in longhand; then define them briefly.

1 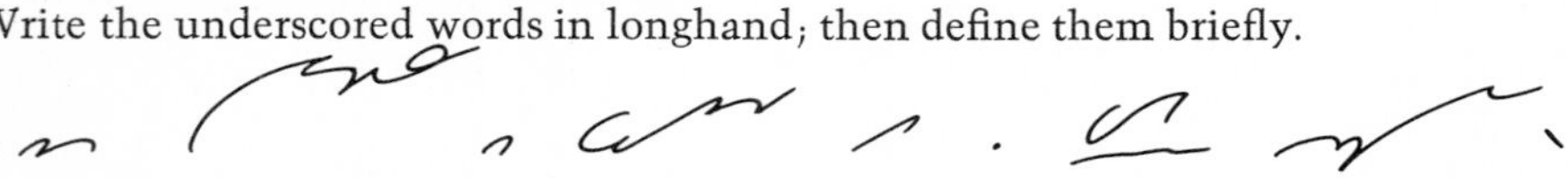

....

2 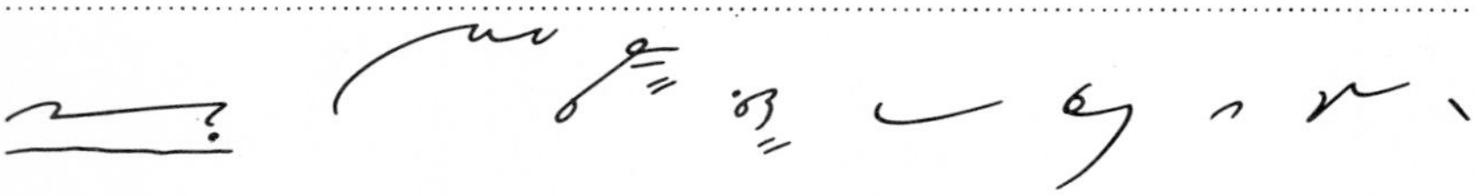

....

3 

....

NAME________________________________ DATE________________

Lesson 23

EVOLUTION DRILLS

In the spaces provided, write the correct shorthand forms.

Brief Forms

1 *time* 	*-s*	*-ing*	*-r*	
2 *acknowledge* 	*-s*	*-ment*	*-ments*	
3 *organize* 	*-s*	*-ing*	*-ation*	
4 *over* 	*-do*	*-see*	*-look*	
5 *general* 	*-s*	*-ly*	*-ize*	
6 *question* 	*-s*	*-ing*	*-ed*	

Words

7 *defeat* 	*-s*	*-ing*	*-ed*
8 *defend* 	*-s*	*-ing*	*-ed*
9 *divide* 	*-s*	*-ing*	*-d*
10 *develop* 	*-s*	*-ing*	*-ment*
11 *devote* 	*-ing*	*-d*	*-s*
12 *create* 	*-s*	*-ing*	*-ive*
13 *negotiate* 	*-s*	*-ing*	*-d*

SPELLING REVIEW

Transcribe the following words in longhand.

1  ....

2  ....

3  ....

4  ....

5  ....

6  ....

7  ....

8  ....

SIMILAR-WORDS DRILL

Define the following words briefly.

to (preposition) ....

too ....

two ....

Transcribe the underscored words in the spaces provided.

1 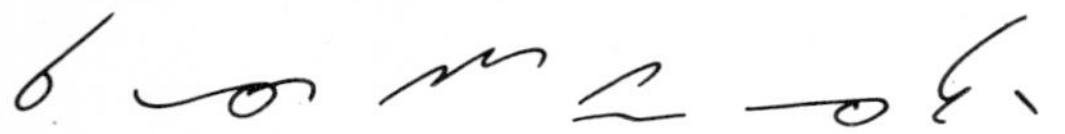 ....

2 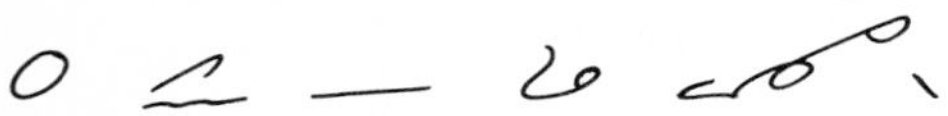 ....

3  ....

4  ....

5 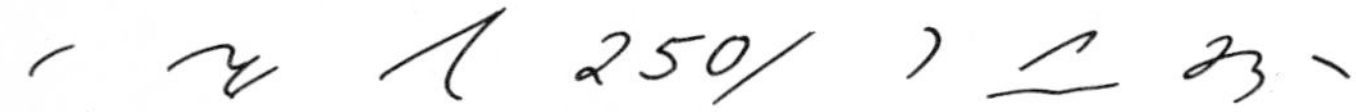 ....

6  ....

BUSINESS VOCABULARY BUILDER

Write the underscored words in longhand; then define them briefly.

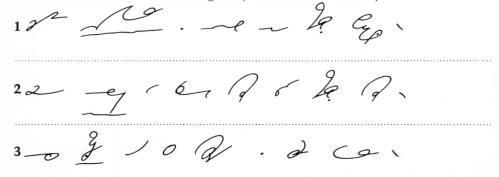

1 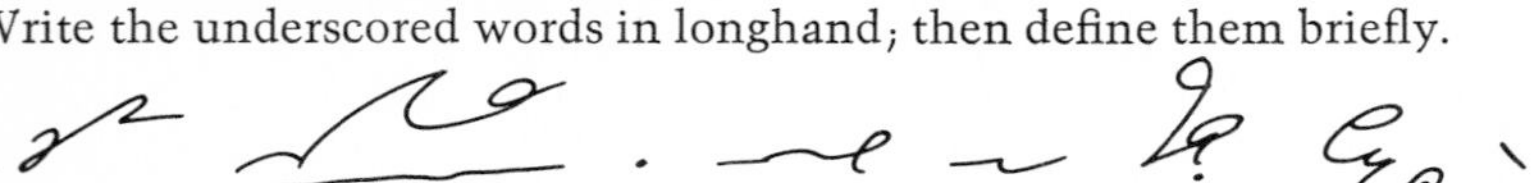

....

2 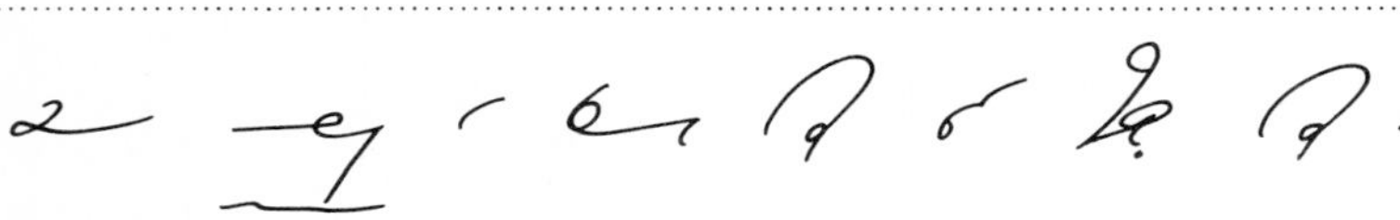

....

3 

....

NAME________________________________ DATE ______________

Lesson 24

RECALL

EVOLUTION DRILLS

In the spaces provided, write the correct shorthand forms.

Brief Forms

1	*present* 	*-ly*	*-s*	*-ed*
2	*advertise* 	*-ing*	*-s*	*-ment*
3	*depart* 	*-s*	*-ing*	*-ed*
4	*suggest* 	*-s*	*-ing*	*-tion*
5	*out* 	*-side*	*-let*	*-fit*
6	*every* 	*-one*	*-day*	*-body*
7	*time* 	*-r*	*-ing*	*-s*
8	*organize* 	*-d*	*-ing*	*-ation*
9	*acknowledge* 	*-d*	*-ing*	*-ment*
10	*overtake* 	*-s*	*-ing*	*-n*

Words

11	*unite* 	*-s*	*-ing*	*-d*
12	*refresh* 	*-ing*	*-ed*	*-ments*
13	*announce* 	*-s*	*-d*	*-ment*

14 *compute*  *-s* *-ing* *-r*

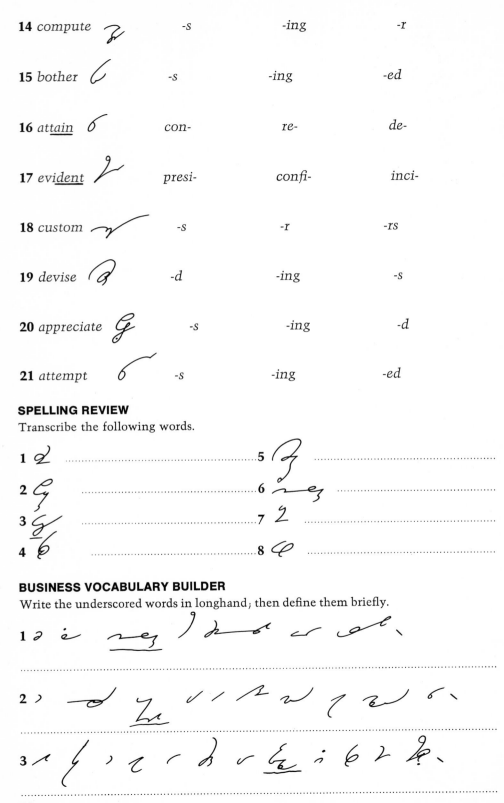

15 *bother*  *-s* *-ing* *-ed*

16 *at<u>tain</u>*  *con-* *re-* *de-*

17 *evi<u>dent</u>*  *presi-* *confi-* *inci-*

18 *custom*  *-s* *-r* *-rs*

19 *devise*  *-d* *-ing* *-s*

20 *appreciate*  *-s* *-ing* *-d*

21 *attempt*  *-s* *-ing* *-ed*

SPELLING REVIEW

Transcribe the following words.

1  ....

2  ....

3  ....

4  ....

5  ....

6  ....

7  ....

8  ....

BUSINESS VOCABULARY BUILDER

Write the underscored words in longhand; then define them briefly.

1 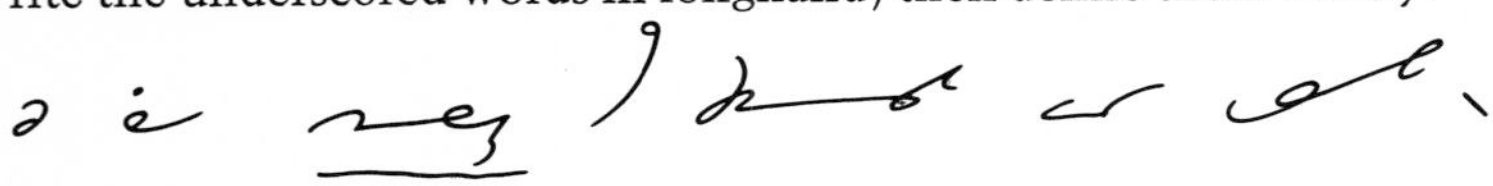

....

2 

....

3 

....

NAME______________________________ DATE______________

Lesson 25

EVOLUTION DRILLS

In the spaces provided, write the correct shorthand forms.

Brief Forms

1 *progress* 	*-s*	*-ed*	*-ive*
2 *satisfy* 	*-s*	*-d*	*-ing*
3 *state* 	*-s*	*-ly*	*-ment*
4 *wish* 	*-s*	*-ing*	*-ed*
5 *under* 	*-stood*	*-stand*	*-line*
6 *difficult* 	*-y*		*-ies*
7 *envelope* 	*-s*	*success* 	*-s*
8 *undertake* 	*-s*	*-ing*	*-n*
9 *request* 	*-s*	*-ing*	*-ed*

Phrases

10 *as soon as* 	*-the*		*-possible*
11 *I hope* 	*-the*	*-that*	*-this*
12 *of course* 	*-it is*	*-it will*	*-it will be*
13 *let us* 	*-see*	*-say*	*-have*
14 *to do* 	*-this*	*-that*	*-the*

Cities and States

15 *New York* *Chicago* *Los Angeles* *St. Louis*

16 *Illinois* *California* *Missouri* *Massachusetts*

Recall

17 *defend* -s -ing -ed

18 *create* -s -ing -d

19 *initial* -s -ing -ed

20 *contain* -s -ing -r

21 *contract* -s -ing -r

22 *commence* -ing -d -ment

23 *amount* -s -ing -ed

SPELLING REVIEW

Transcribe the following words in longhand. Be sure to spell them correctly.

1 .... 5 ....

2 .... 6 ....

3 .... 7 ....

4 .... 8 ....

BUSINESS VOCABULARY BUILDER

Write the underscored words in longhand; then define them briefly.

1 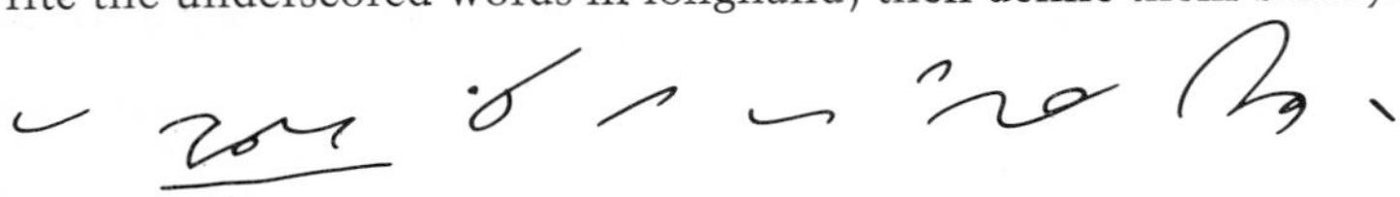

....

2 

....

3 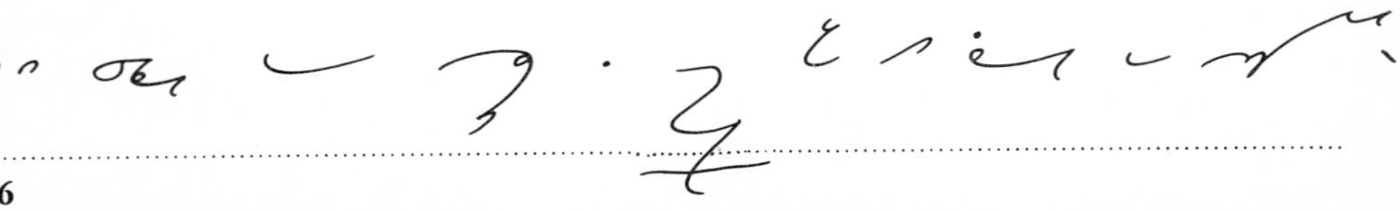

....

NAME______________________________ DATE______________

Lesson 26

EVOLUTION DRILLS

In the spaces provided, write the correct shorthand forms.

1 *apply*		*-s*	*-ing*	*-ance*
2 *rely*		*-s*	*-ing*	*-ance*
3 *dial*		*-s*	*-ing*	*-ed*
4 *unload*		*-ing*	*-s*	*-ed*
5 *unpack*		*-s*	*-ing*	*-ed*
6 *uncertain*		*-paid*	*-signed*	*-settled*
7 *engine*		*-s*	*-eer*	*-eers*
8 *encourage*		*-s*	*-d*	*-ment*
9 *engage*		*-s*	*-ing*	*-ment*
10 *enjoy*		*-s*	*-ing*	*-ment*
11 *encounter*		*-s*	*-ing*	*-ed*
12 *dry*		*-s*	*-ing*	*-er*
13 *diet*		*-s*	*-ing*	*-ed*
14 *endeavor*		*-s*	*-ing*	*-ed*

Recall

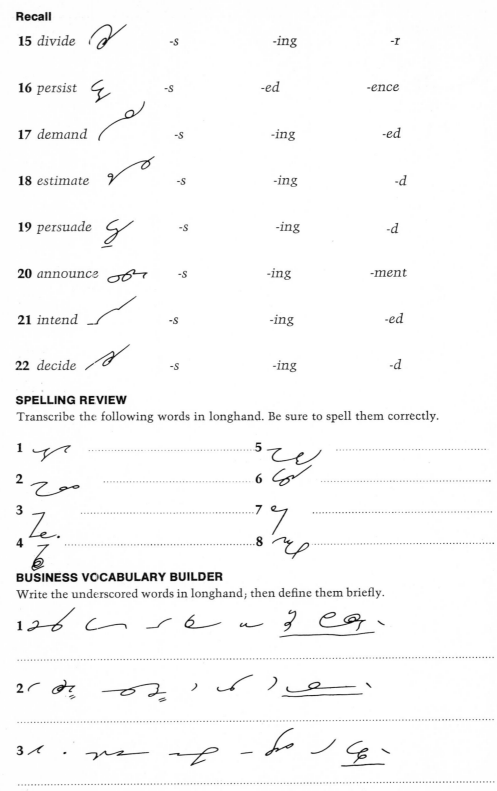

15 *divide*		-s	-ing	-r
16 *persist*		-s	-ed	-ence
17 *demand*		-s	-ing	-ed
18 *estimate*		-s	-ing	-d
19 *persuade*		-s	-ing	-d
20 *announce*		-s	-ing	-ment
21 *intend*		-s	-ing	-ed
22 *decide*		-s	-ing	-d

SPELLING REVIEW

Transcribe the following words in longhand. Be sure to spell them correctly.

1  ....

2  ....

3  ....

4  ....

5  ....

6  ....

7  ....

8  ....

BUSINESS VOCABULARY BUILDER

Write the underscored words in longhand; then define them briefly.

1 

....

2 

....

3 

....

NAME____ DATE____________________

Lesson 27

EVOLUTION DRILLS

In the spaces provided, write the correct shorthand forms.

Brief Forms

1 *speak*	*-ing*	*-s*	*-r*
2 *regard*	*-s*	*-ing*	*-less*
3 *particular* *-ly*	*probable* *-ly*	*regular* *-ly*	
4 *subject*	*-s*	*-ing*	*-ed*
5 *newspaper*	*-s*	*-man*	*-men*

Words

6 *belong*	*-s*	*-ing*	*-ed*
7 *sing*	*-ing*	*-r*	*-rs*
8 *strong*	*-r*	*long*	*-r*
9 *bank*	*-s*	*-ing*	*-r*
10 *drink*	*-s*	*-ing*	*-r*
11 *addition*	*-s*	*-al*	*-ally*
12 *station*	*-s*	*-ed*	*-ery*
13 *commission*	*-s*	*-ed*	*-r*

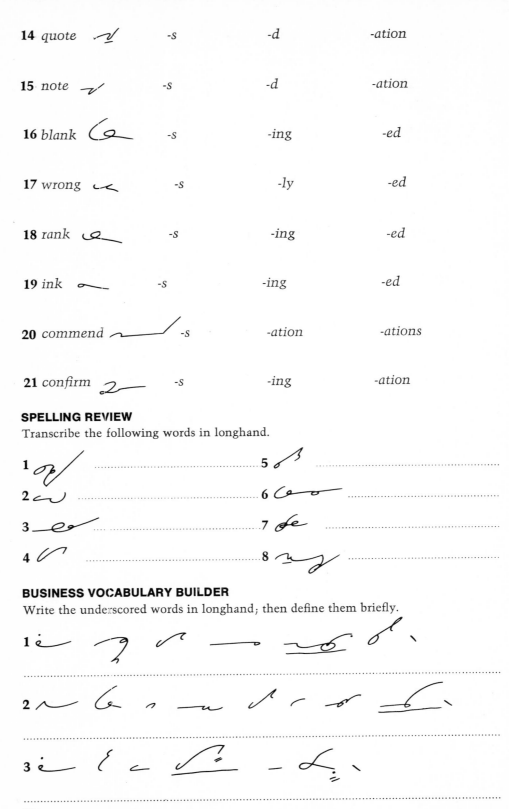

14 *quote*  -s -d -ation

15 *note*  -s -d -ation

16 *blank*  -s -ing -ed

17 *wrong*  -s -ly -ed

18 *rank*  -s -ing -ed

19 *ink*  -s -ing -ed

20 *commend*  -s -ation -ations

21 *confirm*  -s -ing -ation

SPELLING REVIEW

Transcribe the following words in longhand.

1  ....

2  ....

3  ....

4  ....

5  ....

6  ....

7  ....

8  ....

BUSINESS VOCABULARY BUILDER

Write the underscored words in longhand; then define them briefly.

1 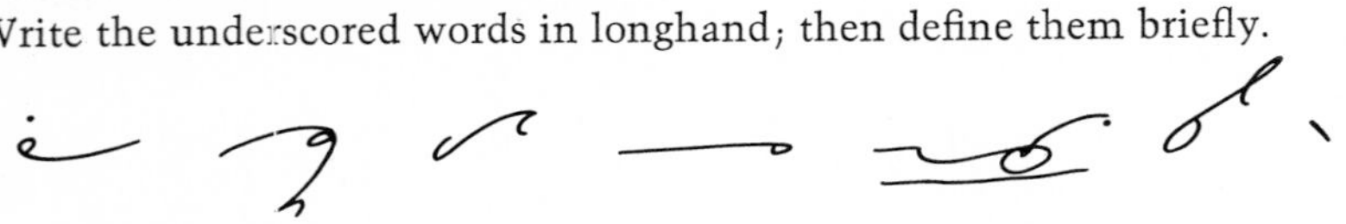

....

2 

....

3 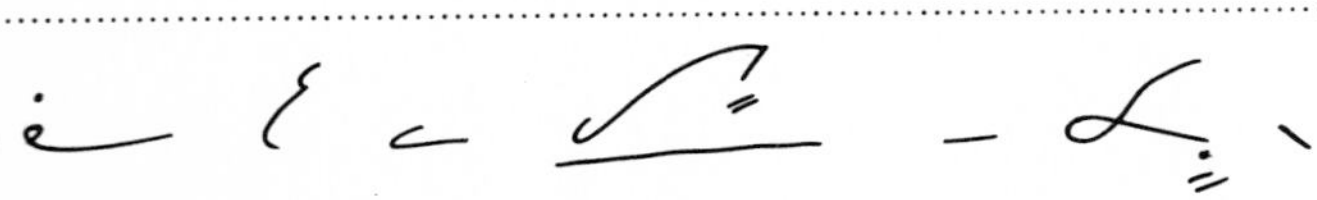

....

NAME______________________________ DATE______________

Lesson 28

EVOLUTION DRILLS

In the spaces provided, write the correct shorthand forms.

1 *await*  *-s* *-ing* *-ed*

2 *awake*  *-s* *-n* *-ning*

3 *award*  *-s* *-ing* *-ed*

4 *tax*  *-ed* *-s* *-ation*

5 *perplex*  *-ed* *-ing* *-s*

6 *relax*  *-s* *-ed* *-ation*

7 *run*  *-s* *-ing* *-r*

8 *refund*  *-s* *-ing* *-ed*

9 *welcome*  *-s* *-ing*

10 *judge*  *-s* *-d* *-ment*

11 *brush*  *-s* *-ed* *-ing*

12 *mix*  *-es* *-ing* *-ed*

13 *index*  *-ing* *-s* *-ed*

14 *fund*  *-s* *-ing* *-ed*

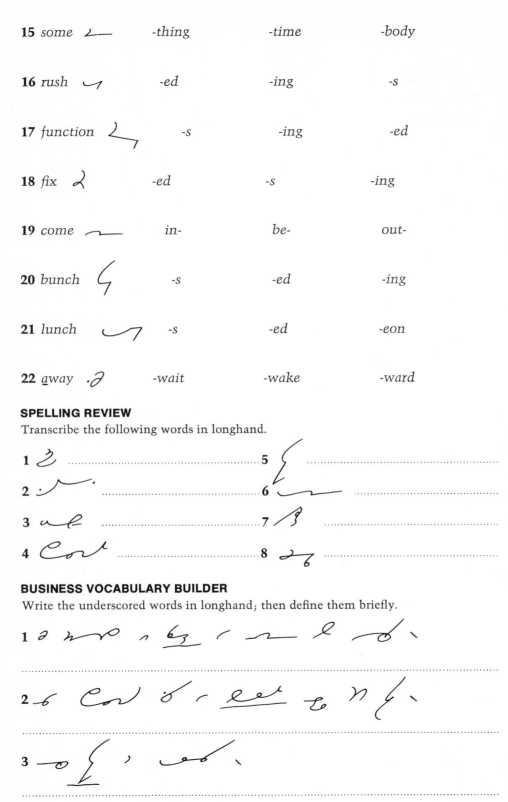

15 *some*  -*thing* -*time* -*body*

16 *rush*  -*ed* -*ing* -*s*

17 *function*  -*s* -*ing* -*ed*

18 *fix*  -*ed* -*s* -*ing*

19 *come* *in*- *be*- *out*-

20 *bunch*  -*s* -*ed* -*ing*

21 *lunch*  -*s* -*ed* -*eon*

22 *away*  -*wait* -*wake* -*ward*

SPELLING REVIEW

Transcribe the following words in longhand.

1  ....

2  ....

3  ....

4  ....

5  ....

6  ....

7  ....

8  ....

BUSINESS VOCABULARY BUILDER

Write the underscored words in longhand; then define them briefly.

1 

....

2 

....

3 

....

NAME______________________________ DATE______________

Lesson 29

EVOLUTION DRILLS

In the spaces provided, write the correct shorthand forms.

Brief Forms

1	*publish*	*-s*	*-ing*	*-ed*
2	*recognize*	*-s*	*-d*	*-ing*
3	*worth*	*-y*	*ordinary*	*-ly*
4	*world*	*-ly*	*public*	*-ly*

Words

5	*expect*	*-s*	*-ed*	*-ation*
6	*excite*	*-s*	*-d*	*-ment*
7	*care*	*-s*	*-d*	*-ful*
8	*thought*	*-less*	*-ful*	*-fully*
9	*help*	*-ed*	*-ful*	*-fully*
10	*chemical*	*-s*	*-ly*	
11	*logical*	*-ly*	*political*	*-ly*
12	*article*	*-s*	*technical*	*-ly*
13	*use*	*-s*	*-ful*	*-fully*

14 *exceed*  -s -ing -ed

15 *expire*  -s -ing -d

16 *delight*  -s -ed -ful

17 *power*  -s -ful -fully

18 *examine*  -s -ing -ation

SIMILAR-WORDS DRILL

Within the parentheses of each of the following sentences insert in longhand either *it's* or *its*—whichever is correct.

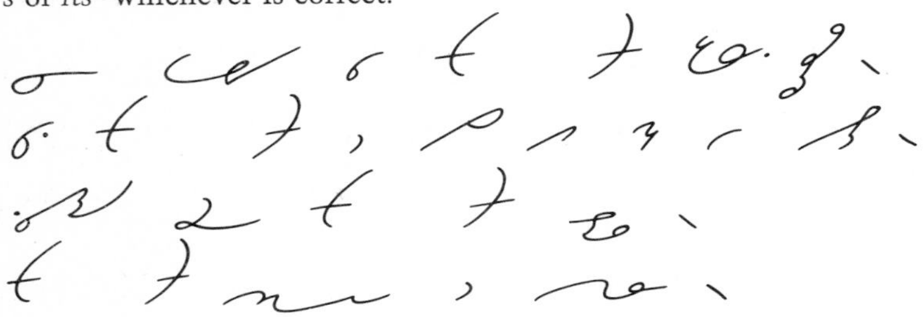

SPELLING REVIEW

Transcribe the following words in longhand.

1  ....

2  ....

3  ....

4  ....

5  ....

6  ....

7  ....

8  ....

BUSINESS VOCABULARY BUILDER

Write the underscored words in longhand; then define them briefly.

1 

....

2 

....

3 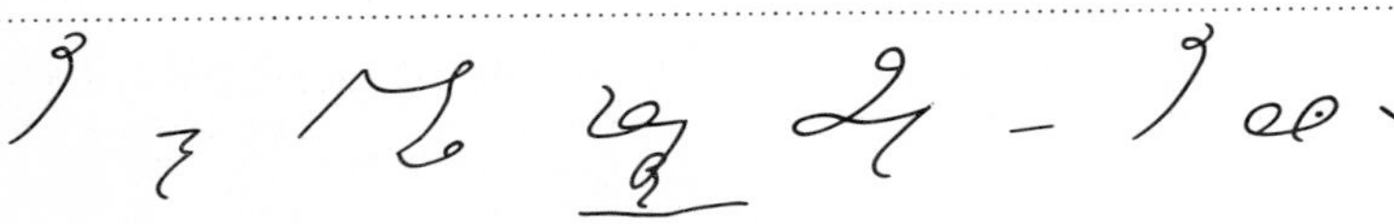

....

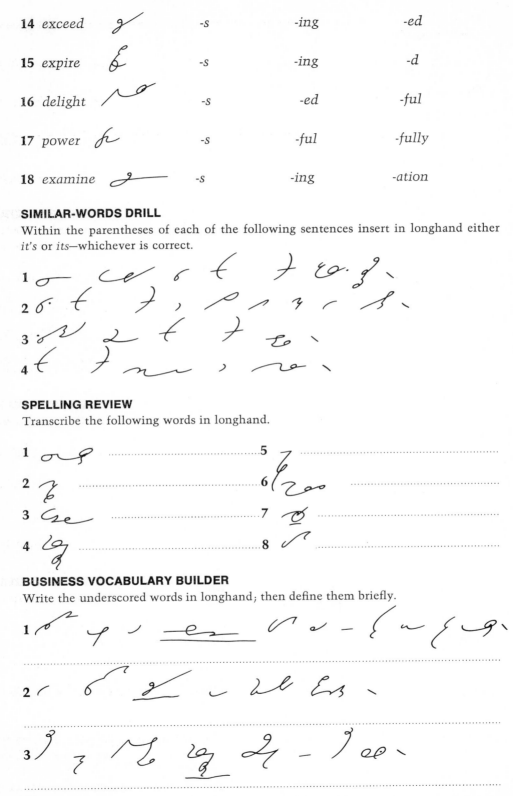

NAME____DATE______________

Lesson 30

RECALL

EVOLUTION DRILLS

In the spaces provided, write the correct shorthand forms.

Brief Forms

1 *success* 	*-s*	*-ful*	*-fully*
2 *request* 	*-s*	*-ing*	*-ed*
3 *progress* 	*-s*	*-ed*	*-ive*
4 *satisfy* 	*-s*	*-d*	*-ing*
5 *under* 	*-go*	*-stand*	*-take*
6 *wish* 	*-ing*	*-ed*	*-ful*
7 *state* 	*-ly*	*-ed*	*-ment*
8 *regard* 	*-s*	*-ing*	*-less*
9 *speak* 	*-ing*	*-r*	*-rs*
10 *recognize* 	*-ing*	*-s*	*-d*
11 *publish* 	*-ed*	*-s*	*-ing*
12 *usual* 	*-ly*	*ordinary* 	*-ly*
13 *experience* 	*-s*	*-ing*	*-d*
14 *newspaper* 	*-s*	*-men*	*-man*

Words

15 *apply*  -s -ing -ance

16 *enjoy*  -s -d -ment

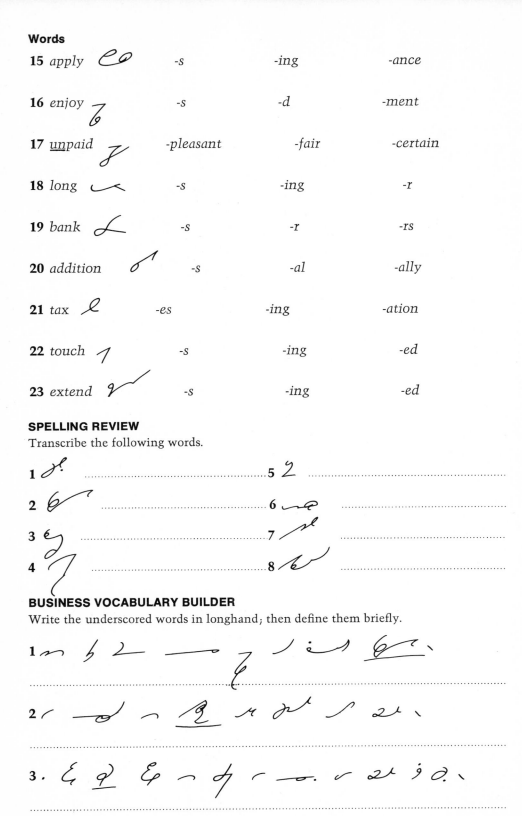

17 *unpaid*  -pleasant -fair -certain

18 *long*  -s -ing -r

19 *bank*  -s -r -rs

20 *addition*  -s -al -ally

21 *tax*  -es -ing -ation

22 *touch*  -s -ing -ed

23 *extend*  -s -ing -ed

SPELLING REVIEW

Transcribe the following words.

1  ....

5  ....

2  ....

6  ....

3  ....

7  ....

4  ....

8  ....

BUSINESS VOCABULARY BUILDER

Write the underscored words in longhand; then define them briefly.

1 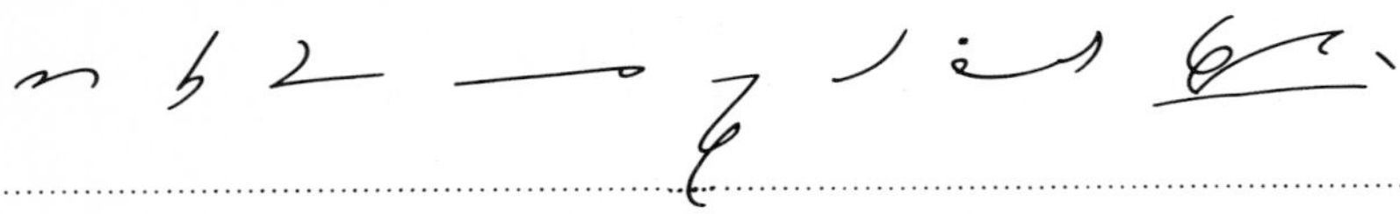

....

2 

....

3. 

....

PART 2

Lessons 31-70

Practice suggestions

PUNCTUATION AND SPELLING DRILLS

In Part 2 you will give considerable attention to improving your ability to spell and to punctuate. You will do this through the Spelling and Punctuation Drills, which consist of sentences in shorthand adapted from the Reading and Writing Practice exercises of your textbook. After you have read and copied a Reading and Writing Practice exercise from your textbook, practice the corresponding Punctuation and Spelling Drill in this way:

1 Read an entire sentence aloud. If you cannot immediately read an outline, spell it. If the spelling does not give you the outline, encircle it and find out its meaning in class the next day. Do not spend more than a few seconds trying to decipher any outline.

2 Insert the proper punctuation in shorthand.

3 In the space provided at the right of the page, under "Reason for Punctuation," give the reason for the punctuation you have used. To save time, you may use the following abbreviations.

1	, parenthetical	, par	6	, *when* clause	, when
2	, apposition	, ap	7	, *as* clause	, as
3	, series	, ser	8	, conjunction	, conj
4	, introductory	, intro	9	, *and* omitted	, and o
5	, *if* clause	, if			

A summary of the punctuation rules you will study in *Gregg Shorthand, Series 90,* is given in the back of this workbook.

4 Some of the shorthand outlines have small encircled numbers above them. Write these words in longhand in the spaces provided at the bottom of the page.

Example

In the workbook you will find: **Reason for Punctuation**

1 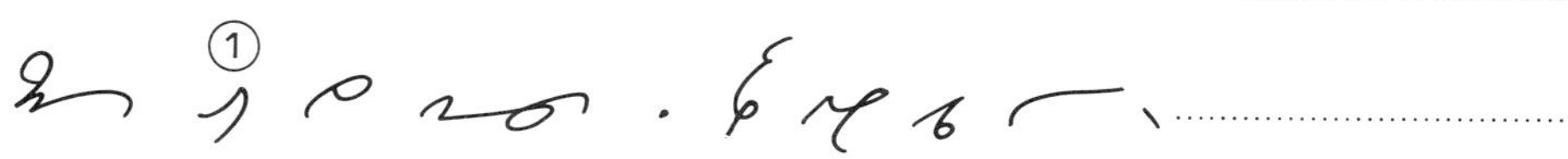

The completed drill will look like this:

1 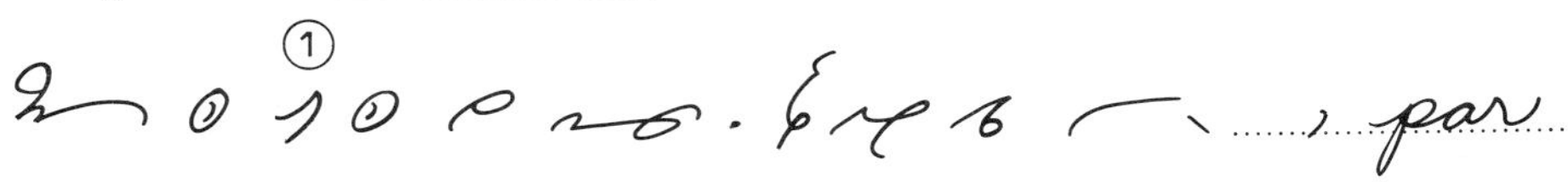

The word *therefore* will then be spelled in longhand next to the number *1* under the heading "Spelling Words."

OTHER DRILLS

Suggestions for practicing the other types of drills in Part 2 are given at the point where the drills are first introduced.

TIME GOALS

Here are some time goals for you to shoot at in Part 2.

Lessons 31 through 36	12 minutes
Lessons 37 through 42	10 minutes
Lessons 43 through 48	9 minutes
Lessons 49 through 54	8 minutes
Lessons 55 through 70	7 minutes

If you can complete these lessons in less time, you are making fine progress indeed.

NAME____ DATE____________________

Lesson 31

EVOLUTION DRILLS

In the spaces provided, write the correct shorthand forms.

Brief Forms

1 *quantity*  *-s* *executive*  *-s*

2 *object*  *-s* *-ing* *-ive*

3 *govern*  *-s* *-ment* *-or*

4 *correspond*  *-s* *-ing* *-ed*

Words

5 *picture*  *-s* *-d* *-esque*

6 *fix*  *-s* *-ing* *-ture*

7 *proceed*  *-s* *-ure* *-ures*

8 *equal*  *-s* *-ed* *-ize*

9 *schedule*  *-s* *-ing* *-d*

10 *manual*  *-s* *-ly*

11 *feature*  *-s* *-ing* *-d*

12 *expend*  *-s* *-ed* *-iture*

13 *venture*  *-s* *-ing* *-d*

14 *gradual*  *-ly* *actual*  *-ly*

15 *nature*  *-al* *-ally*

16 *secure*  *-s* *-ing* *-d*

PUNCTUATION AND SPELLING

Punctuate the following sentences and write in longhand the spelling words indicated. Follow the directions on page 69.

Reason for Punctuation

Spelling Words

1 .... 6 ....

2 .... 7 ....

3 .... 8 ....

4 .... 9 ....

5 .... 10 ....

NAME________________________________ DATE________________

Lesson 32

EVOLUTION DRILLS

In the spaces provided, write the correct shorthand forms.

1	*speed*		*-s*	*-y*		*-ily*
2	*haste*		*-ily*	*heavy*		*-ily*
3	*alter*		*-s*	*-ing*		*-ation*
4	*dispute*		*-s*	*-ing*		*-d*
5	*discover*		*-s*	*-ing*		*-ed*
6	*describe*		*-s*	*-ing*		*-d*
7	*though*		*al-*	*together*		*al-*
8	*discourage*		*-d*	*-ing*		*-ment*
9	*displace*		*-ing*	*-d*		*-ment*
10	*temporary*		*-ily*	*hearty*		*-ily*
11	*disturb*		*-s*	*-ing*		*-ed*
12	*easy*		*-ily*	*ready*		*-ily*
13	*destroy*		*-s*	*-ing*		*-ed*
14	*dispose*		*-ing*	*-s*		*-d*

PUNCTUATION AND SPELLING

Punctuate the following sentences and write in longhand the spelling words indicated. Follow the directions on page 69.

Reason for Punctuation

Spelling Words

1 ......

2 ......

3 ......

4 ......

5 ......

6 ......

7 ......

8 ......

9 ......

10 ......

NAME____ DATE____________________

Lesson 33

EVOLUTION DRILLS

In the spaces provided, write the correct shorthand forms.

1 *afford*  *-s* *-ing* *-ed*

2 *effort*  *-s* *-less* *-lessly*

3 *inform*  *-s* *-ing* *-ation*

4 *furnish*  *-s* *-ing* *-ed*

5 *enforce*  *-s* *-d* *-ment*

6 *comfort*  *-s* *-ble* *-bly*

7 *forgive*  *-s* *-ing* *-n*

8 *further*  *-s* *-ing* *-more*

9 *refurnish*  *-s* *-ing* *-ed*

10 *conform*  *-s* *-ing* *-ation*

Phrases

11 *several months ago*  *-days ago* *-minutes ago*

12 *few days ago*  *-months* *-minutes*

13 *days ago*  *weeks-* *years-*

14 *to forget*  *-form* *-furnish* *-force*

PUNCTUATION AND SPELLING

Punctuate the following sentences and write in longhand the spelling words indicated. Follow the directions on page 69.

Reason for Punctuation

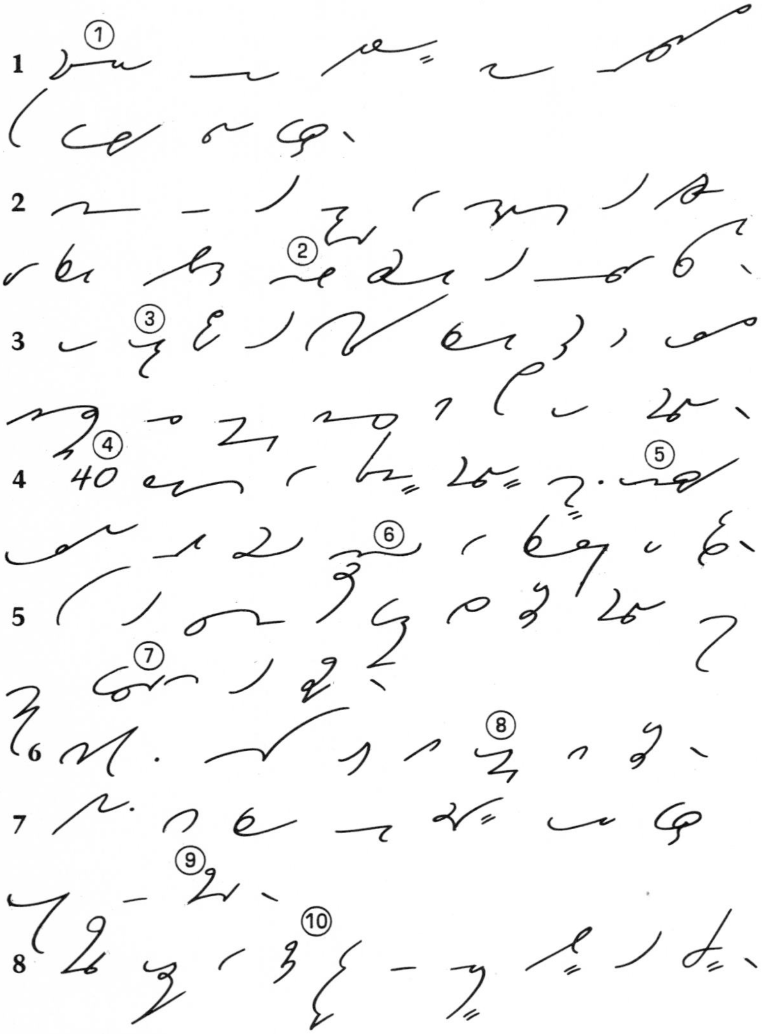

Spelling Words

1 .... 6 ....

2 .... 7 ....

3 .... 8 ....

4 .... 9 ....

5 .... 10 ....

NAME____________________ DATE____________

Lesson 34

EVOLUTION DRILLS

In the spaces provided, write the correct shorthand forms.

Phrases

1 *they want*  *you-* *we-* *I-*

2 *he wanted*  *we-* *you-* *who-*

Words

3 *term*  *-s* *-ing* *-ed*

4 *frame*  *-s* *-ing* *-d*

5 *report*  *-s* *-ed* *-r*

6 *export*  *-s* *-ing* *-ation*

7 *determine*  *-s* *-ing* *-ation*

8 *inform*  *-s* *-ation* *-ed*

9 *return*  *-s* *-ing* *-ed*

10 *modernize*  *-ing* *-s* *-d*

11 *claim*  *-s* *-ing* *-ed*

12 *prompt*  *-ly* *-ness*

13 *terminate*  *-s* *-ing* *-d*

14 *quarter*  *-s* *-ly*

PUNCTUATION AND SPELLING

Punctuate the following sentences and write in longhand the spelling words indicated. Follow the directions on page 69.

Reason for Punctuation

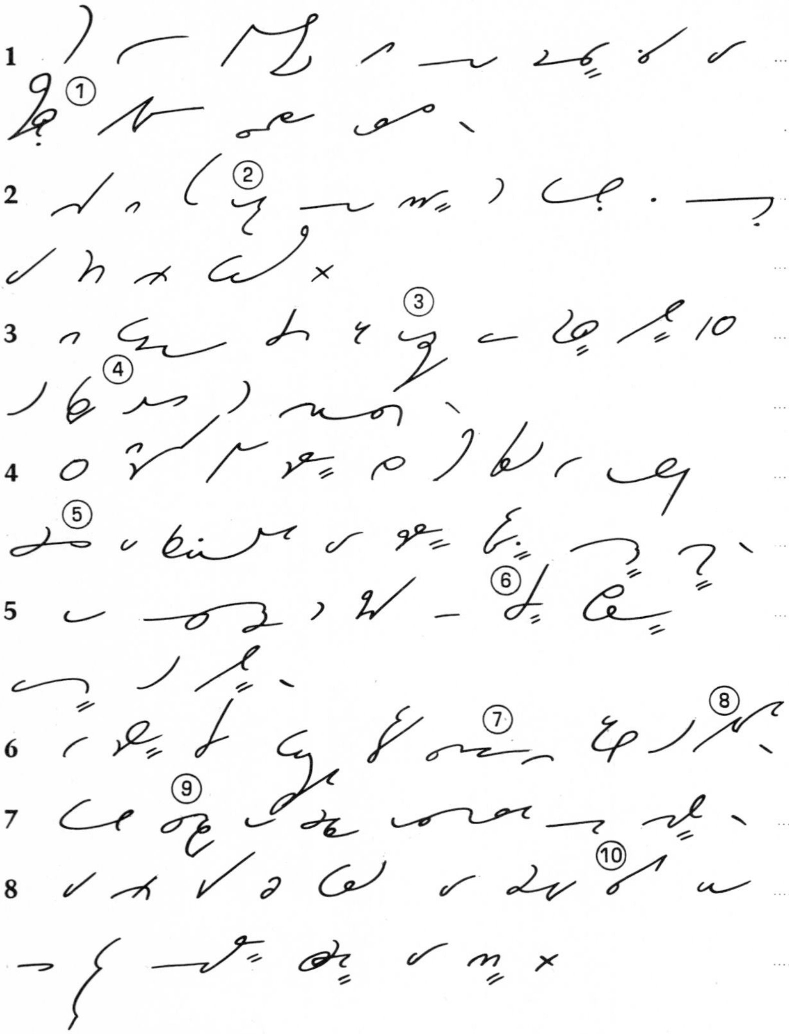

Spelling Words

1 .... 6 ....

2 .... 7 ....

3 .... 8 ....

4 .... 9 ....

5 .... 10 ....

NAME________________________________ DATE________________

Lesson 35

EVOLUTION DRILLS

In the spaces provided, write the correct shorthand forms.

1 *interest* 	*-ing*	*-ed*	*-s*
2 *interview* 	*-s*	*-ed*	*-ing*
3 *introduce* 	*-ing*	*-d*	*-s*
4 *entertain* 	*-s*	*-ing*	*-ed*
5 *hold* 	*-s*	*-ing*	*-ings*
6 *deal* 	*-s*	*-r*	*-ings*
7 *interrupt* 	*-ed*	*-s*	*-ing*
8 *enter*	*-s*	*-ing*	*-ed*
9 *interfere* 	*-s*	*-ing*	*-ence*
10 *proceed* 	*-s*	*-ed*	*-ings*

Phrases

11 *some of the* 	*-these*	*-them*	*-our*
12 *out of them* 	*-the*	*-these*	*-that*
13 *none of them* 	*-these*	*-our*	*-the*
14 *one of these* 	*-our*	*-them*	*-the*

PUNCTUATION AND SPELLING

Punctuate the following sentences and write in longhand the spelling words indicated. Follow the directions on page 69.

Reason for Punctuation

Spelling Words

1

2

3

4

5

6

7

8

9

10

NAME ____________________ DATE ____________

Lesson 36

RECALL

SIMILAR-WORDS DRILL

Define the following words briefly:

addition ....

edition ....

Within the parentheses in each of the following sentences, write in longhand either *addition* or *edition*—whichever is correct.

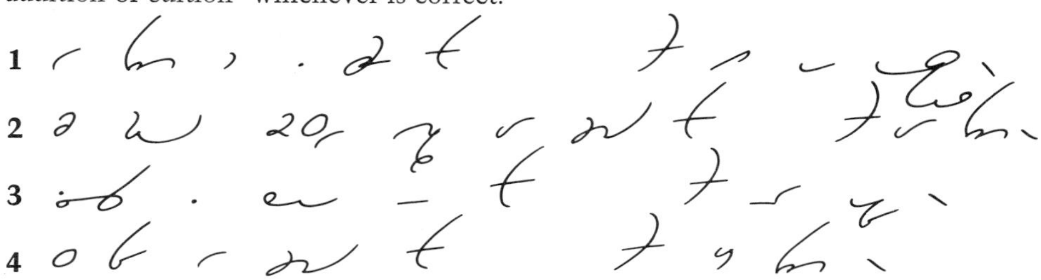

BUSINESS VOCABULARY BUILDER

Write the underscored words in longhand; then define them briefly.

1 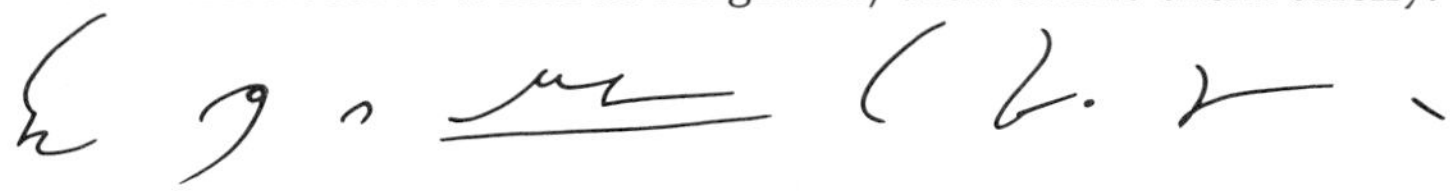

....

2 

....

3 

....

4 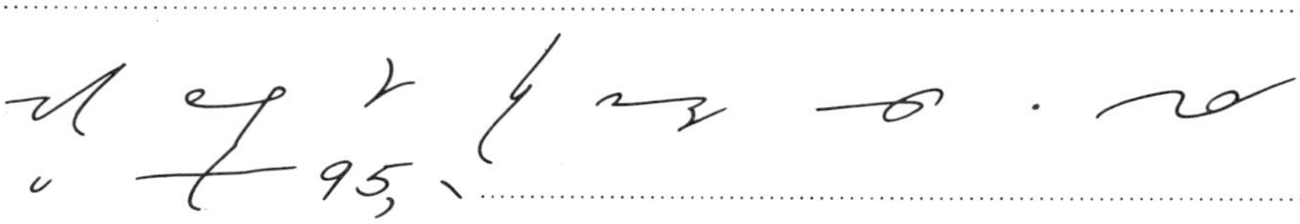

....

5 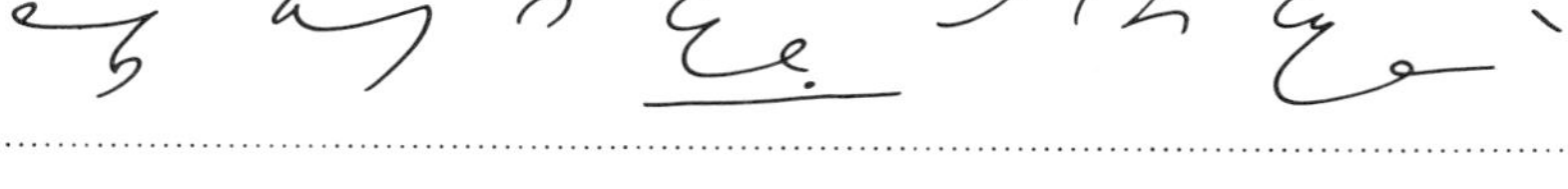

....

PUNCTUATION AND SPELLING

Punctuate the following sentences and write in longhand the spelling words indicated. Follow the directions on page 69.

Reason for Punctuation

Spelling Words

1 .... 6 ....

2 .... 7 ....

3 .... 8 ....

4 .... 9 ....

5 .... 10 ....

NAME____DATE____________________

Lesson 37

EVOLUTION DRILLS

In the spaces provided, write the correct shorthand forms.

1 *increase*  *-d* *-ing* *-ingly*

2 *amaze*  *-d* *-ing* *-ingly*

3 *interest*  *-ed* *-ing* *-ingly*

4 *impress*  *-ed* *-ing* *-ive*

5 *import*  *-s* *-ed* *-ation*

6 *employ*  *-s* *-ing* *-r*

7 *embarrass*  *-ed* *-ing* *-ment*

8 *situate*  *-s* *-d* *-ing*

9 *courteous*  *-ly* *serious*  *-ly*

10 *previous*  *-ly* *tedious*  *-ly*

11 *exceed*  *-s* *-ed* *-ingly*

12 *improve*  *-s* *-d* *-ment*

13 *seem*  *-s* *-ed* *-ingly*

14 *imprint*  *-s* *-ing* *-ed*

PUNCTUATION AND SPELLING

Punctuate the following sentences and write in longhand the spelling words indicated. Follow the directions on page 69.

Reason for Punctuation

Spelling Words

1 .... 6 ....

2 .... 7 ....

3 .... 8 ....

4 .... 9 ....

5 .... 10 ....

NAME ____________________ DATE ____________

Lesson 38

EVOLUTION DRILLS

In the spaces provided, write the correct shorthand forms.

1	*steam*	*-ing*	*-r*	*-ship*
2	*relation*	*-s*	*-ship*	*-ships*
3	*submit*	*-s*	*-ing*	*-ed*
4	*subscribe*	*-s*	*-ing*	*-d*
5	*regulate*	*-s*	*-ing*	*-d*
6	*formulate*	*-s*	*-ing*	*-d*
7	*regulation*	*circ-*	*congrat-*	*stim-*
8	*majority*	*-s*	*minority*	*-s*
9	*security*	*-s*	*charity*	*-s*
10	*fellowship*	*leader-*	*member-*	*friend-*
11	*subdivide*	*-s*	*-ing*	*-d*
12	*congratulate*	*-ing*	*-s*	*-d*
13	*calculate*	*-ing*	*-d*	*-r*
14	*substantial*	*-ly*	*subdivision*	*-s*

PUNCTUATION AND SPELLING

Punctuate the following sentences and write in longhand the spelling words indicated. Follow the directions on page 69.

Reason for Punctuation

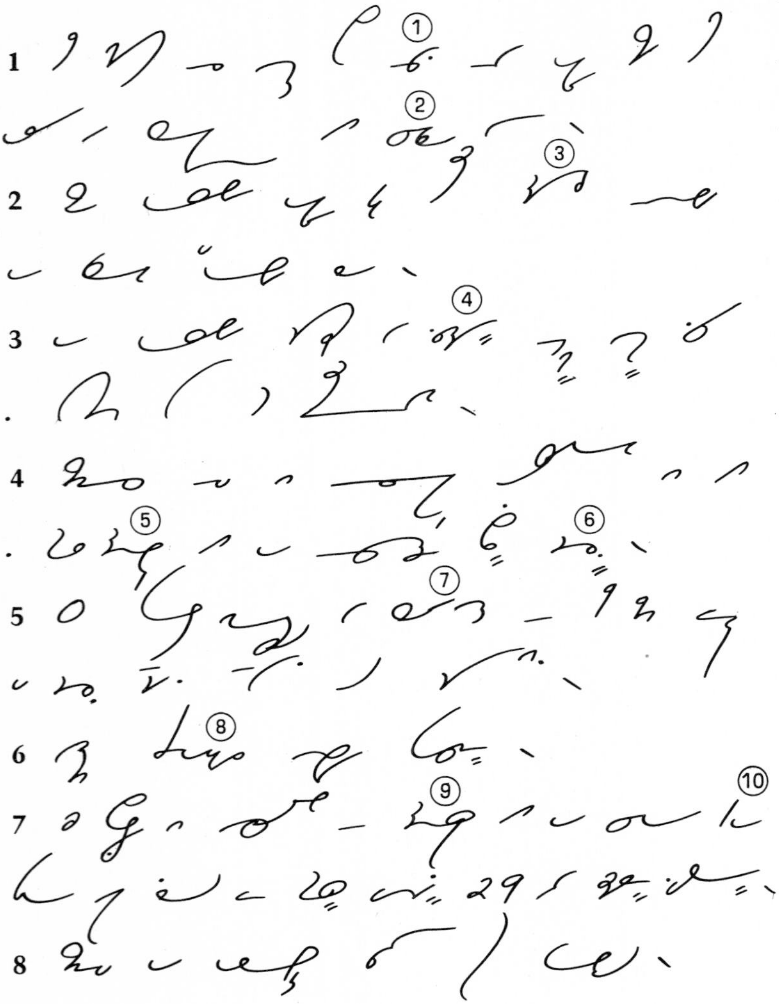

Spelling Words

1 ____________________ 6 ____________________

2 ____________________ 7 ____________________

3 ____________________ 8 ____________________

4 ____________________ 9 ____________________

5 ____________________ 10 ____________________

NAME________________________________ DATE______________

Lesson 39

EVOLUTION DRILLS

In the spaces provided, write the correct shorthand forms.

1	*ability*	*-s*	*locality*	*-s*	
2	*person*	*-s*	*-al*	*-ality*	
3	*faculty*	*-s*	*penalty*	*-s*	
4	*facility*	*-s*	*authority*	*-s*	
5	*quality*	*-s*	*utility*	*-s*	
6	*herself*	*him-*	*my-*	*it-*	
7	*ourselves*	*them-*	*your-*		

Recall

8	*friend*	*-s*	*-ly*	*-ship*	
9	*stimulate*	*-ing*	*-d*	*-s*	
10	*congratulate*	*-ing*	*-s*	*-d*	
11	*convince*	*-s*	*-d*	*-ingly*	
12	*substantial*	*-ly*	*impartial*	*-ly*	
13	*embarrass*	*-ed*	*-s*	*-ment*	
14	*serious*	*-ly*	*-ness*		

PUNCTUATION AND SPELLING

Punctuate the following sentences and write in longhand the spelling words indicated. Follow the directions on page 69.

Reason for Punctuation

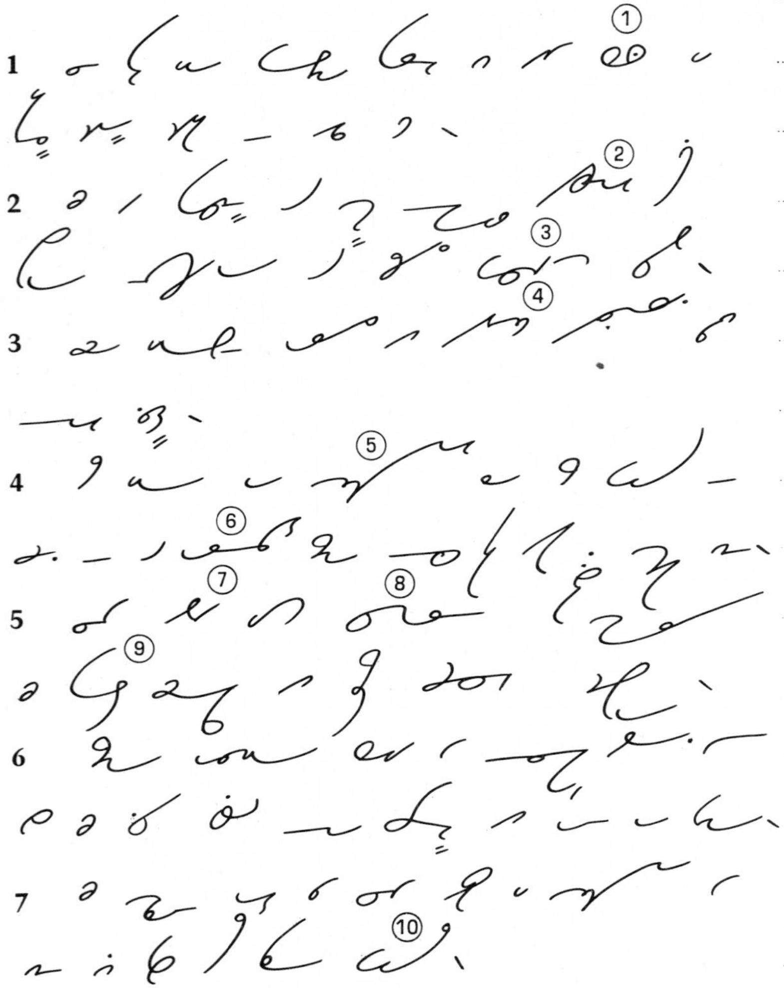

Spelling Words

1 .... 6 ....

2 .... 7 ....

3 .... 8 ....

4 .... 9 ....

5 .... 10 ....

NAME________________________________ DATE______________

Lesson 40

EVOLUTION DRILLS

In the spaces provided, write the correct shorthand forms.

1 *require* -d -ing -ment

2 *inquire* -s -ing -d

3 *substitute* -s -ing

4 *attribute* -s -ing -d

5 *contribute* -d -ing -s

6 *aptitude* -s *attitude* -s

7 *frequent* -ly *consequent* -ly

8 *subsequent* -ly *eloquent* -ly

9 *distribute* -ing -d -r

10 *constitute* -s -ing

Recall

11 *yourself* *my-* *him-* *her-*

12 *submit* -s -ed -ing

13 *security* -s *majority* -s

14 *ability* -s *liability* -s

PUNCTUATION AND SPELLING

Punctuate the following sentences and write in longhand the spelling words indicated. Follow the directions on page 69.

Reason for Punctuation

Spelling Words

1 ....
2 ....
3 ....
4 ....
5 ....
6 ....
7 ....
8 ....
9 ....
10 ....

NAME______________________________ DATE________________

Lesson 41

EVOLUTION DRILLS

In the spaces provided, write the correct shorthand forms.

1 *telegraph*  *-s* *-ing* *-ed*

2 *autograph*  *-s* *-ing* *-ed*

3 *statistic*  *-s* *memorandum*  *-s*

4 *privilege*  *-s* *-d*

5 *transact*  *-ed* *-s* *-ing*

6 *transport*  *-s* *-ed* *-ation*

7 *transfer*  *-s* *-ed* *-ence*

8 *convenient*  *-ly* *reluctant*  *-ly*

9 *photograph*  *-s* *-ed* *-r*

10 *transmit*  *-s* *-ing* *-ed*

Recall

11 *contribute*  *-s* *-d* *-r*

12 *require*  *-d* *-s* *-ment*

13 *lead*  *-s* *-r* *-rship*

14 *circulate*  *-ing* *-s* *-r*

PUNCTUATION AND SPELLING

Punctuate the following sentences and write in longhand the spelling words indicated. Follow the directions on page 69.

Reason for Punctuation

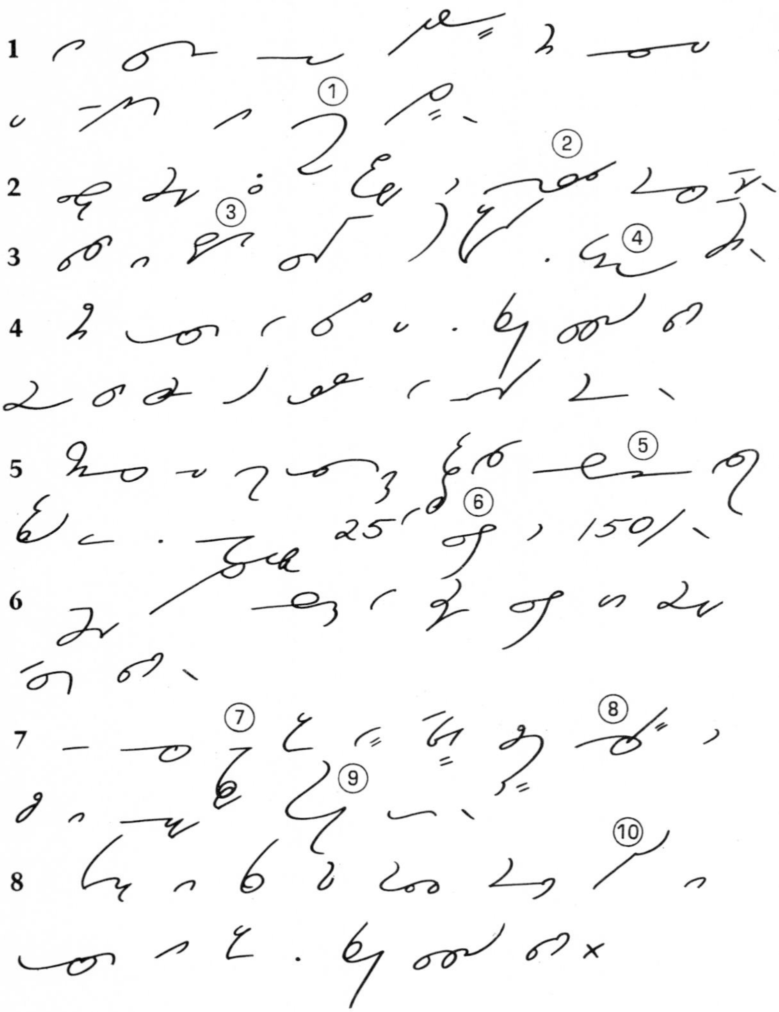

Spelling Words

1 .... 6 ....

2 .... 7 ....

3 .... 8 ....

4 .... 9 ....

5 .... 10 ....

NAME______________________________ DATE______________

Lesson 42

RECALL

SIMILAR-WORDS DRILL

Define the following words briefly:

assistance ....

assistants ....

Within the parentheses of each of the following sentences, write in longhand either *assistance* or *assistants*—whichever is correct.

1 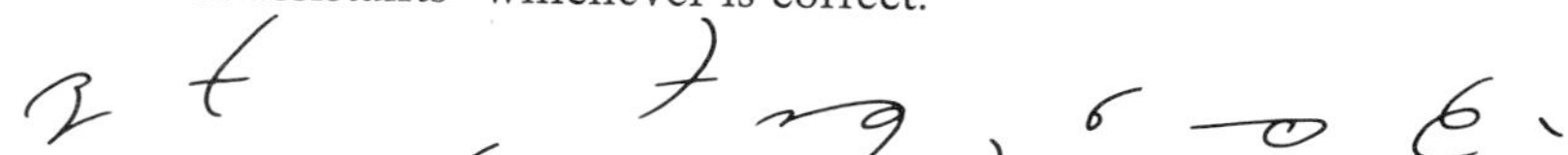

2 

3 

4 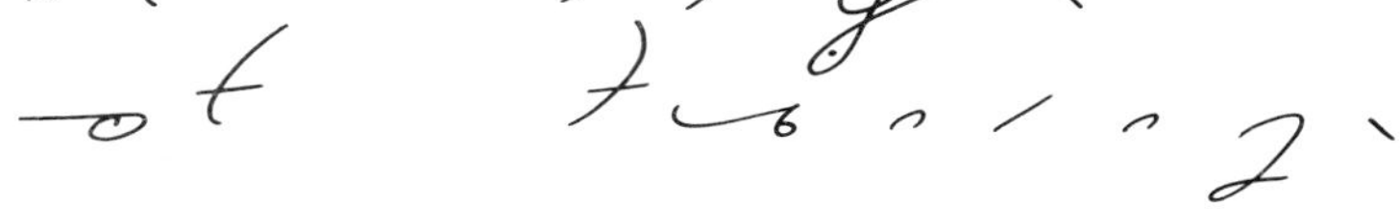

BUSINESS VOCABULARY BUILDER

Write the underscored words in longhand; then define them briefly.

1 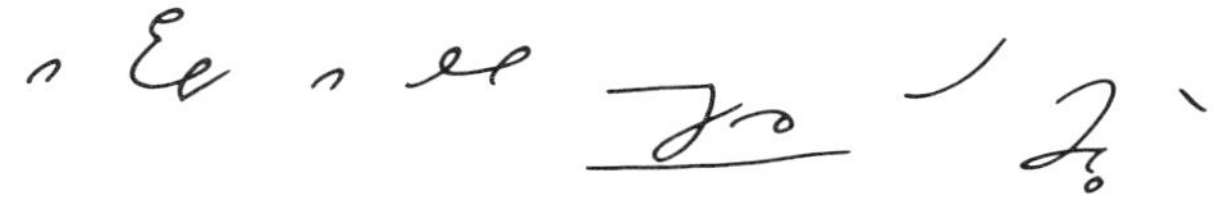

....

2 

....

3 

....

4 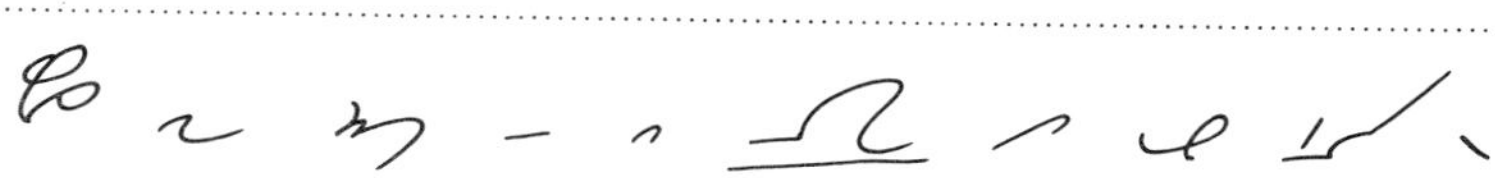

....

....

5 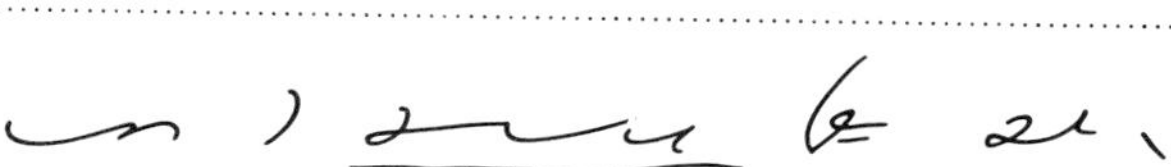

....

PUNCTUATION AND SPELLING

Punctuate the following sentences and write in longhand the spelling words indicated. Follow the directions on page 69.

Reason for Punctuation

Spelling Words

1 ....

2 ....

3 ....

4 ....

5 ....

6 ....

7 ....

8 ....

9 ....

10 ....

NAME________________________________ DATE________________

Lesson 43

EVOLUTION DRILLS

In the spaces provided, write the correct shorthand forms.

1 *mistake*  *-s* *-n* *-nly*

2 *misplace*  *-d* *-s* *-ing*

3 *misunderstand*  *-s* *-ing* *-ings*

4 *supervise*  *-ing* *-r* *-d*

5 *superintend*  *-ing* *-s* *-ent*

6 *mutual*  *-ly* *musical*  *-ly*

7 *continue*  *-s* *-ing* *-d*

8 *discontinue*  *-s* *-ing* *-ance*

9 *communicate*  *-s* *-ing* *-d*

10 *misinform*  *-s* *-ing* *-ation*

11 *translate*  *-ing* *-d* *-r*

12 *contribute*  *-s* *-ing* *-r*

13 *tabulate*  *-s* *-ing* *-r*

14 *hard<u>ship</u>*  *author-* *steam-* *friend-*

PUNCTUATION AND SPELLING

Punctuate the following sentences and write in longhand the spelling words indicated. Follow the directions on page 69.

Reason for Punctuation

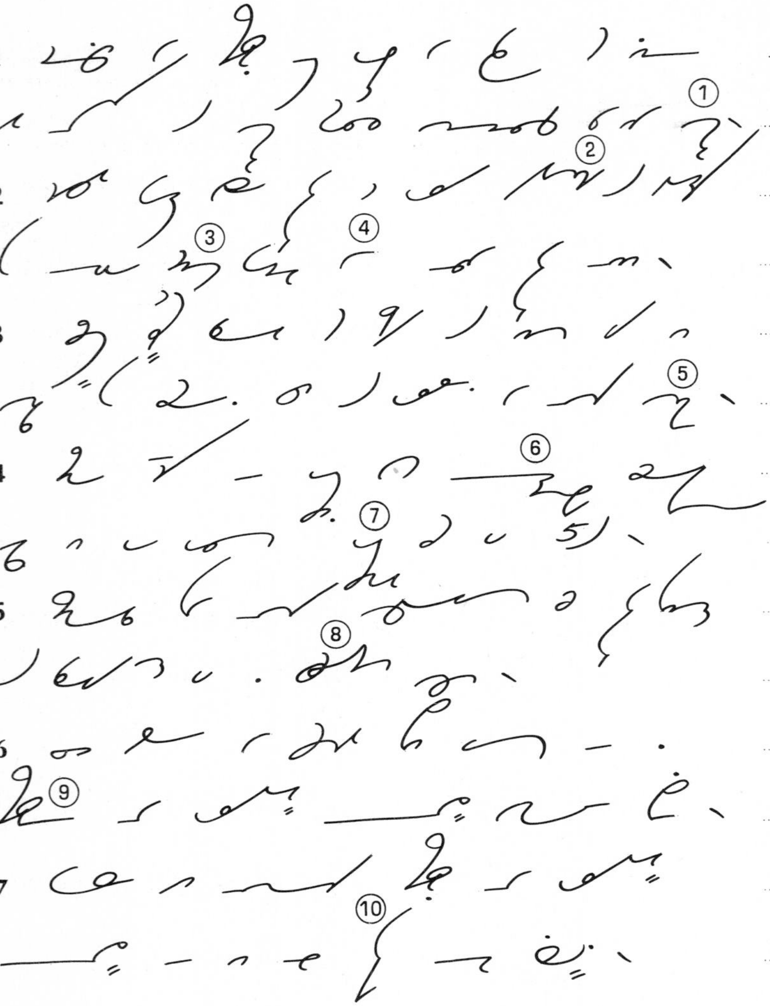

1 ....
....

2 ....
....

3 ....
....

4 ....
....

5 ....
....

6 ....
....

7 ....
....

Spelling Words

1 .... 6 ....

2 .... 7 ....

3 .... 8 ....

4 .... 9 ....

5 .... 10 ....

NAME________________________________ DATE________________

Lesson 44

EVOLUTION DRILLS

In the spaces provided, write the correct shorthand forms.

1 *class* *-s* *-ed* *-ification*

2 *note* *-d* *-s* *-ification*

3 *circumstance* *-s* *qualification* *-s*

4 *self-made* *-confidence* *-reliance* *-addressed*

5 *selfish* *-ly* *-ness*

6 *circumvent* *-s* *-ed* *-ing*

7 *just* *-ice* *-ly* *-ification*

8 *circumnavigate* *-s* *-ation*

Recall

9 *continue* *-s* *-ing* *-d*

10 *supervise* *-r* *-ing* *-d*

11 *misinform* *-s* *-ing* *-ation*

12 *autograph* *-ed* *telegraph* *-ed*

13 *transcribe* *-d* *-s* *-ing*

14 *utility* *-s* *authority* *-s*

PUNCTUATION AND SPELLING

Punctuate the following sentences and write in longhand the spelling words indicated. Follow the directions on page 69.

Reason for Punctuation

Spelling Words

1 .... 6 ....

2 .... 7 ....

3 .... 8 ....

4 .... 9 ....

5 .... 10 ....

NAME________________________________ DATE________________

Lesson 45

EVOLUTION DRILLS

In the spaces provided, write the correct shorthand forms.

1	*neighborhood*	*child-*	*boy-*	*parent-*
2	*like*	*-s*	*-ly*	*-lihood*
3	*backward*	*on-*	*after-*	*out-*
4	*reward*	*-s*	*-ing*	*-ed*
5	*forward*	*-s*	*-ing*	*-ed*
6	*result*	*-s*	*-ing*	*-ed*
7	*multiply*	*-s*	*-ing*	*-d*
8	*consult*	*-s*	*-ed*	*-ation*
9	*culture*	*-s*	*-d*	*-al*
10	*culminate*	*-s*	*-ing*	*-d*
11	*adult*	*-s*	*-hood*	

QUANTITIES

12	*$600*	*5,000,000*	*$1,000,000*	*$5,000,000,000*
13	*a pound*	*-dollar*	*-foot*	*-hundred*
14	*several hundred*	*-million*	*-feet*	*-pounds*

PUNCTUATION AND SPELLING

Punctuate the following sentences and write in longhand the spelling words indicated. Follow the directions on page 69.

Reason for Punctuation

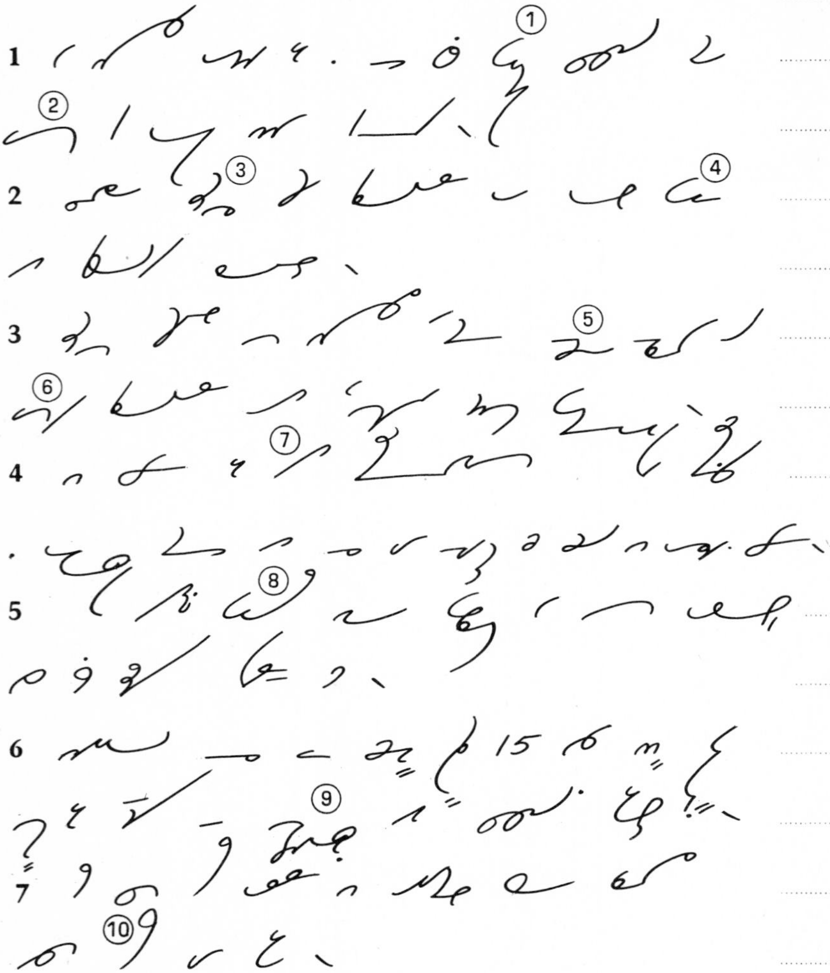

Spelling Words

1 ....

2 ....

3 ....

4 ....

5 ....

6 ....

7 ....

8 ....

9 ....

10 ....

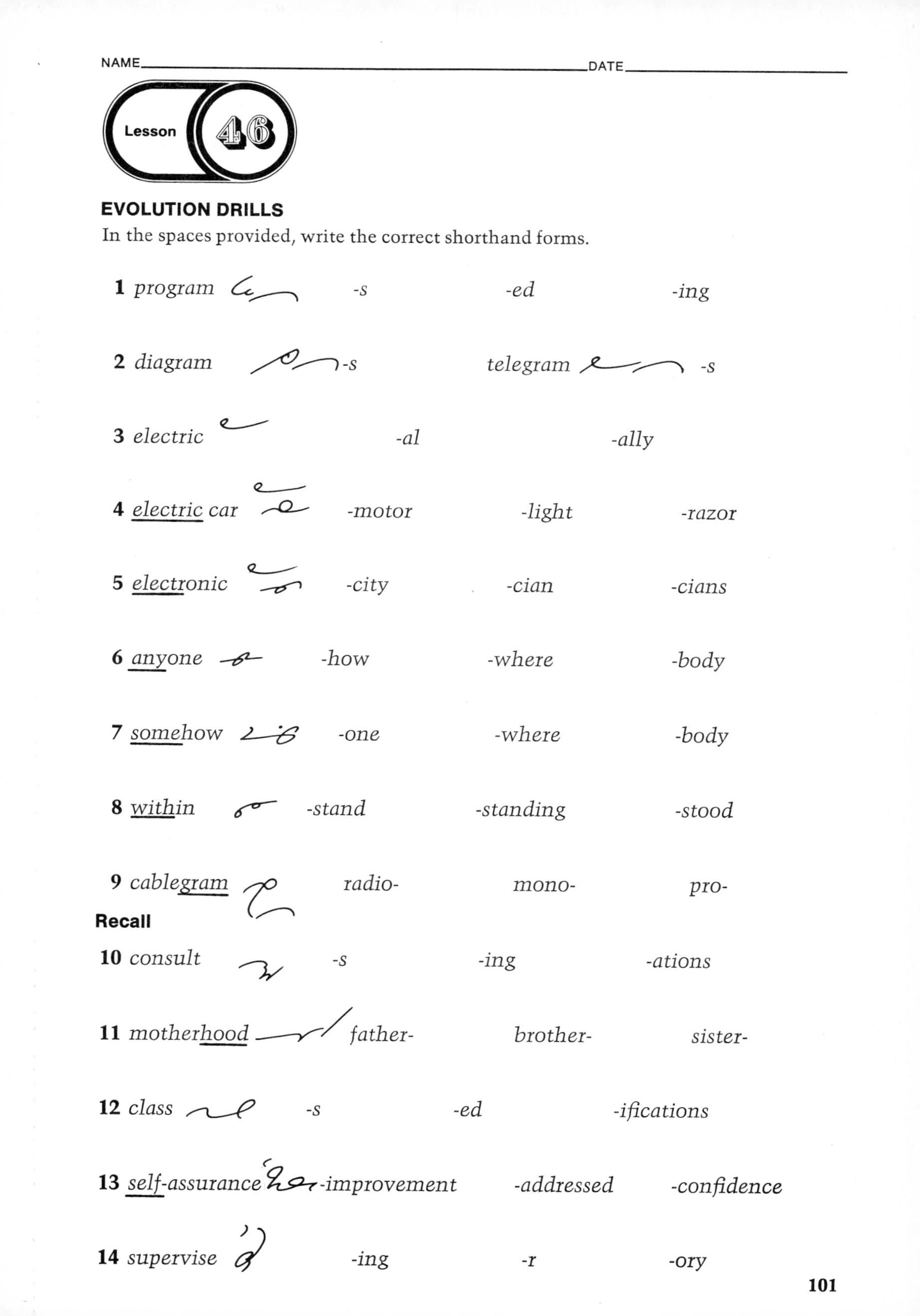

NAME ______________________________ DATE ______________

Lesson 46

EVOLUTION DRILLS

In the spaces provided, write the correct shorthand forms.

1 *program*   *-s*   *-ed*   *-ing*

2 *diagram*   *-s*   *telegram*   *-s*

3 *electric*   *-al*   *-ally*

4 *electric car*   *-motor*   *-light*   *-razor*

5 *electronic*   *-city*   *-cian*   *-cians*

6 *anyone*   *-how*   *-where*   *-body*

7 *somehow*   *-one*   *-where*   *-body*

8 *within*   *-stand*   *-standing*   *-stood*

9 *cablegram*   *radio-*   *mono-*   *pro-*

Recall

10 *consult*   *-s*   *-ing*   *-ations*

11 *motherhood*   *father-*   *brother-*   *sister-*

12 *class*   *-s*   *-ed*   *-ifications*

13 *self-assurance*   *-improvement*   *-addressed*   *-confidence*

14 *supervise*   *-ing*   *-r*   *-ory*

PUNCTUATION AND SPELLING

Punctuate the following sentences and write in longhand the spelling words indicated. Follow the directions on page 69.

Reason for Punctuation

Spelling Words

1 .... 6 ....

2 .... 7 ....

3 .... 8 ....

4 .... 9 ....

5 .... 10 ....

NAME____ DATE____________________

Lesson 47

EVOLUTION DRILLS

In the spaces provided, write the correct shorthand forms.

1 *Pittsburgh* *Harris-* *Platts-* *Greens-*

2 *Buckingham* *Nott-* *Cunn-* *Fram-*

3 *Lexington* *Wilm-* *Bloom-* *Wash-*

4 *Brownsville* *Nash-* *Jackson-* *Evans-*

Recall

5 *cablegram* *pro-* *dia-* *mono-*

6 *electric light* *-typewriter* *-calculator* *-motor*

7 *onward* *out-* *back-* *for-*

8 *insult* *-s* *-ing* *-ed*

9 *self-assured* *-reliance* *-satisfaction* *-made*

10 *modification* *-s* *specification* *-s*

11 *translate* *-d* *-s* *-ing*

12 *privilege* *-s* *-d*

13 *himself* *her-* *my-* *your-*

14 *formulate* *-s* *-ing* *-d*

PUNCTUATION AND SPELLING

Punctuate the following sentences and write in longhand the spelling words indicated. Follow the directions on page 69.

Reason for Punctuation

Spelling Words

1 ……………… 6 ………………

2 ……………… 7 ………………

3 ……………… 8 ………………

4 ……………… 9 ………………

5 ……………… 10 ………………

NAME____DATE____________________

Lesson 48

RECALL

SPELLING FAMILIES

Transcribe the following words.

1  ....

2  ....

3  ....

4  ....

5  ....

6  ....

SIMILAR-WORDS DRILL

Define the following words briefly.

prominent ....

permanent ....

Within the parentheses in each of the following sentences, insert in longhand either *prominent* or *permanent*—whichever is correct.

1 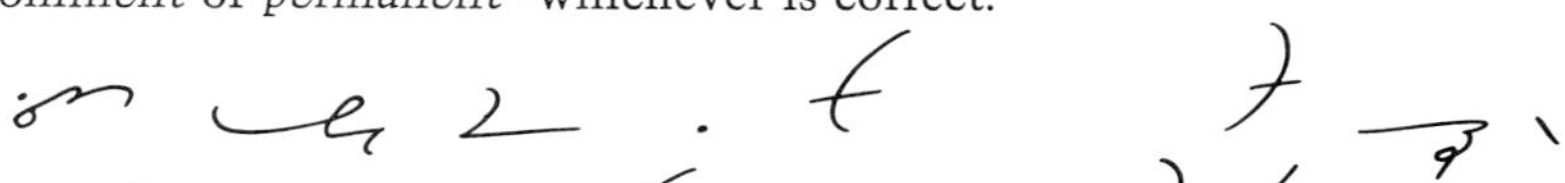

2 

3 

4 

BUSINESS VOCABULARY BUILDER

Write the underscored words in longhand; then define them briefly.

1 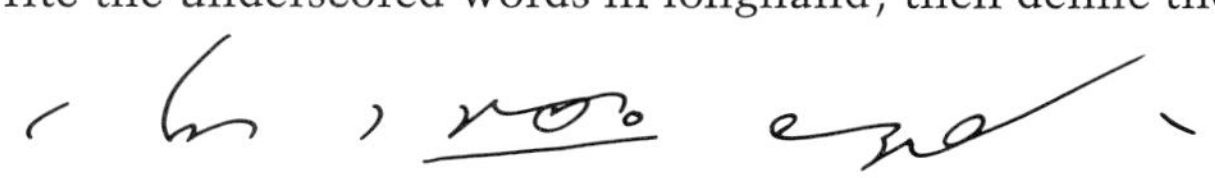

....

2 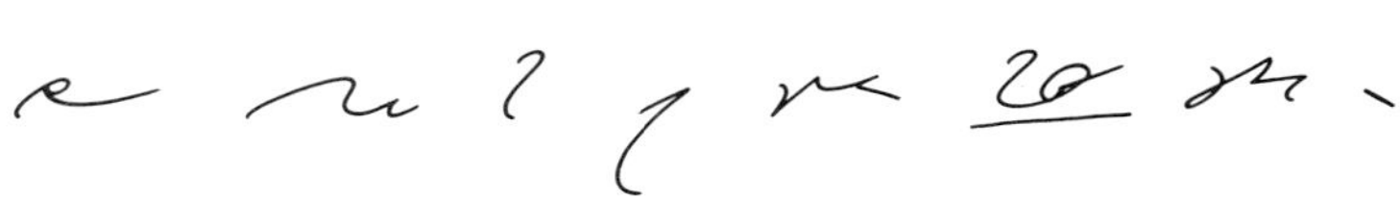

....

3 

....

PUNCTUATION AND SPELLING

Punctuate the following sentences and write in longhand the spelling words indicated. Follow the directions on page 69.

Reason for Punctuation

Spelling Words

1 .... 6 ....

2 .... 7 ....

3 .... 8 ....

4 .... 9 ....

5 .... 10 ....

NAME____ DATE____________________

Lesson 49

EVOLUTION DRILLS

In the spaces provided, write the correct shorthand forms.

1 *serve* 	-s	-ing	-d	
2 *hit* 	-s	-ing	-r	
3 *earn* 	-ing	-s	-r	
4 *throw* 	-s	-ing	-n	
5 *give* 	-s	-ing	-n	
6 *risk* 	-s	-ing	-ed	
7 *step* 	-s	-ing	-ed	
8 *settle* 	-ing	-s	-rs	
9 *bid* 	-s	-ing	-r	
10 *farm* 	-s	-r	-rs	
11 *ride* 	-s	-ing	-r	
12 *prove* 	-s	-ing	-d	
13 *wait* 	-s	-ing	-r	
14 *cool* 	-s	-ing	-r	

15 *make*  *-s* *-ing* *-r*

16 *arrive*  *-s* *-ing* *-d*

17 *pack*  *-s* *-ing* *-ed*

18 *invest*  *-s* *-ing* *-r*

19 *big*  *-r* *-est* *-ness*

20 *learn*  *-s* *-r* *-rs*

21 *thick*  *-r* *-ness* *-est*

22 *surprise*  *-ing* *-d*

23 *fill*  *-s* *-ing* *-r*

Phrases

24 *we have*  *-will* *-are* *-may*

25 *I can*  *-will* *-am* *-know*

26 *in the*  *to-* *at-* *if-*

27 *to go*  *-get* *-tell* *-try*

28 *of these*  *-our* *-the* *-my*

29 *you may*  *-will* *-have* *-can*

30 *who are*  *-will* *-can* *-know*

NAME____ DATE______________________

Lesson 50

EVOLUTION DRILLS

In the spaces provided, write the correct shorthand forms.

1 *ship*  -s -ing -ed

2 *search*  -s -ing -ed

3 *charge*  -s -ing -d

4 *lock*  -s -ing -ed

5 *authorize*  -ing -s -d

6 *believe*  -ing -s -d

7 *cost*  -s -ing -ly

8 *caution*  -s -ing -ed

9 *friend*  -s -ly -liness

10 *print*  -s -ing -r

11 *increase*  -ing -d -s

12 *hard*  -r -ness -ly

13 *bill*  -s -ing -ed

14 *mail*  -s -ing -ed

15 *fold*  -s -ing -r

16 *store*  -s -ing -d

17 *prevent*  -s -ing -ed

18 *lately*  like- slight- sure-

Phrases

19 *will be*  would- can- should-

20 *this can*  -is -may -would

21 *to pay*  -please -play -plan

22 *after them*  -the -that -which

23 *from that*  -the -this -which

24 *have been*  you- I- we-

25 *to be able*  should- will- would-

BUSINESS VOCABULARY BUILDER

Write the underscored words in longhand; then define them briefly.

1 

....

2 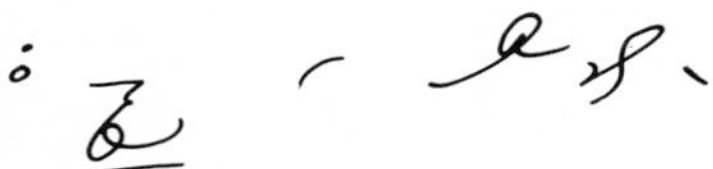

....

3 

....

NAME____ DATE____________________

Lesson 51

EVOLUTION DRILLS

In the spaces provided, write the correct shorthand forms.

1 *adjust*  *-s* *-ing* *-ed*

2 *cook*  *-s* *-ing* *-ed*

3 *equip*  *-s* *-ing* *-ed*

4 *study*  *-s* *-ing* *-d*

5 *agree*  *-s* *-d* *-ble*

6 *reason*  *-s* *-ing* *-ble*

7 *mention*  *-s* *-ing* *-ed*

8 *yield*  *-s* *-ing* *-ed*

9 *join*  *-s* *-ing* *-ed*

10 *persuade*  *-s* *-ing* *-d*

11 *purchase*  *-ing* *-r* *-rs*

12 *deposit*  *-s* *-r* *-rs*

13 *direct*  *-ing* *-r* *-rs*

14 *accept*  *-s* *-ed* *-ble*

15 *look*  *-s* *-ing* *-ed*

16 *quote*  *-s* *-ing* *-d*

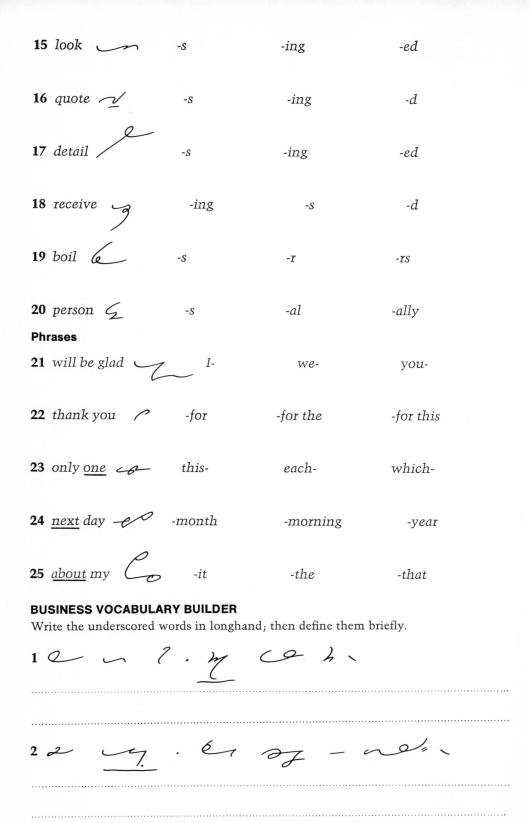

17 *detail*  *-s* *-ing* *-ed*

18 *receive*  *-ing* *-s* *-d*

19 *boil*  *-s* *-r* *-rs*

20 *person*  *-s* *-al* *-ally*

Phrases

21 *will be glad*  *I-* *we-* *you-*

22 *thank you*  *-for* *-for the* *-for this*

23 *only one*  *this-* *each-* *which-*

24 *next day*  *-month* *-morning* *-year*

25 *about my*  *-it* *-the* *-that*

BUSINESS VOCABULARY BUILDER

Write the underscored words in longhand; then define them briefly.

1 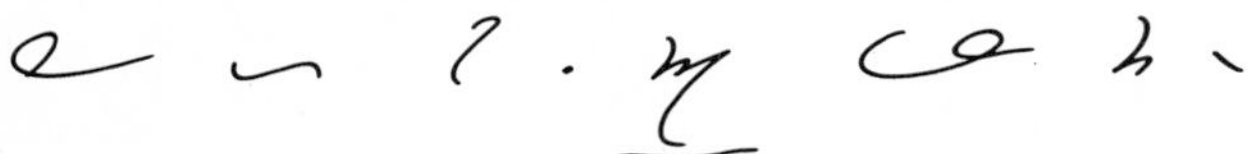

....

....

2 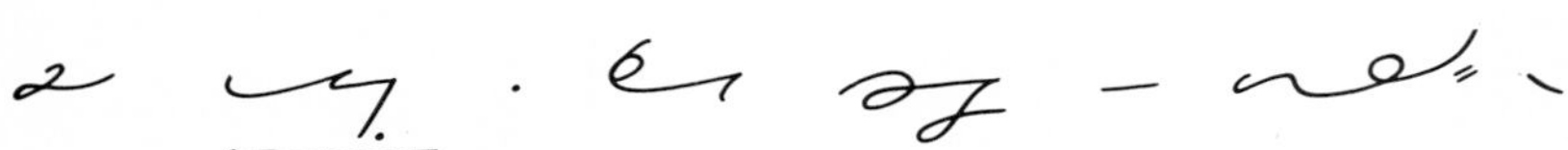

....

....

NAME____DATE____________________

Lesson 52

EVOLUTION DRILLS

In the spaces provided, write the correct shorthand forms.

1	*review*		*-s*	*-ing*	*-ed*
2	*announce*		*-s*	*-d*	*-ment*
3	*gather*		*-s*	*-ing*	*-ed*
4	*concern*		*-s*	*-ing*	*-ed*
5	*complete*		*-s*	*-ing*	*-d*
6	*compute*		*-d*	*-r*	*-rs*
7	*incident*		*-s*	*-al*	*-ally*
8	*intend*		*-s*	*-ed*	*-ing*
9	*remit*		*-s*	*-ing*	*-ance*
10	*contain*		*-s*	*-r*	*-rs*
11	*attempt*	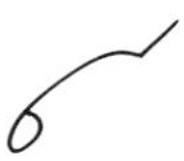	*-s*	*-ing*	*-ed*
12	*custom*		*-r*	*-rs*	*-ary*
13	*create*		*-s*	*-ing*	*-r*
14	*develop*		*-s*	*-ment*	*-ments*

15 *divide* -s -d -r

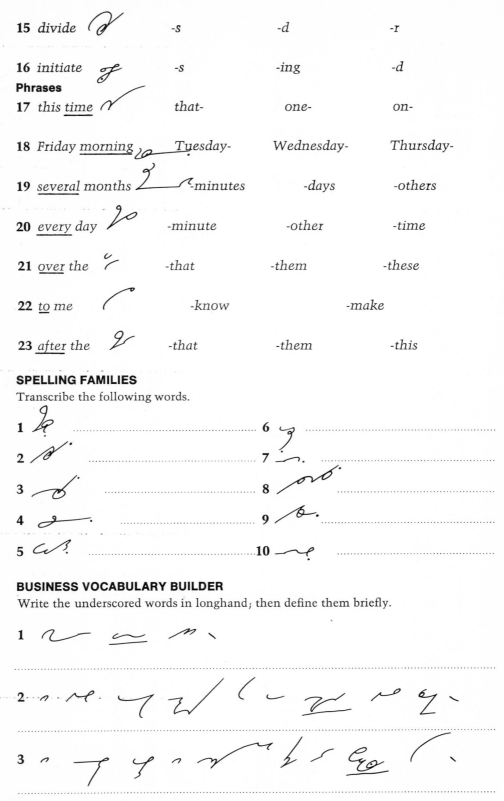

16 *initiate* -s -ing -d

Phrases

17 *this time* that- one- on-

18 *Friday morning* Tuesday- Wednesday- Thursday-

19 *several months* -minutes -days -others

20 *every day* -minute -other -time

21 *over the* -that -them -these

22 *to me* -know -make

23 *after the* -that -them -this

SPELLING FAMILIES

Transcribe the following words.

1 ....

2 ....

3 ....

4 ....

5 ....

6 ....

7 ....

8 ....

9 ....

10 ....

BUSINESS VOCABULARY BUILDER

Write the underscored words in longhand; then define them briefly.

1 

....

2 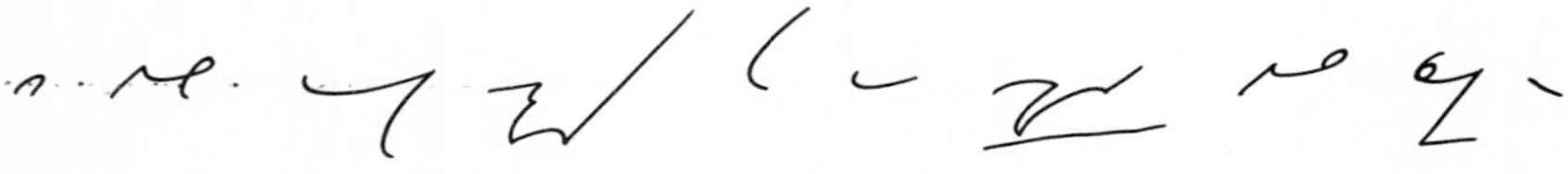

....

3 

....

NAME________________________________ DATE________________

Lesson 53

EVOLUTION DRILLS

In the spaces provided, write the correct shorthand forms.

1 *dial*	*-s*	*-ing*	*-ed*
2 *unpack*	*-s*	*-ing*	*-ed*
3 *enjoy*	*-s*	*-ble*	*-ment*
4 *sing*	*-s*	*-ing*	*-r*
5 *bank*	*-s*	*-r*	*-rs*
6 *quote*	*-s*	*-d*	*-ation*
7 *tax*	*-ed*	*-s*	*-ation*
8 *come*	*in-*	*be-*	*out-*
9 *excite*	*-d*	*-ing*	*-ment*
10 *logical*	*-ly*	*surgical*	*-ly*
11 *doubt*	*-s*	*-ing*	*-ful*
12 *thought*	*-s*	*-less*	*-ful*
13 *await*	*-s*	*-ing*	*-ed*
14 *engage*	*-s*	*-d*	*-ment*

Phrases

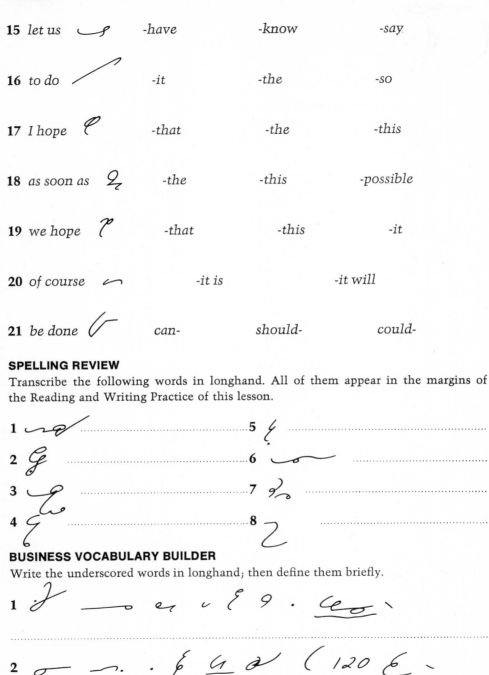

15 *let us* — *-have* — *-know* — *-say*

16 *to do* — *-it* — *-the* — *-so*

17 *I hope* — *-that* — *-the* — *-this*

18 *as soon as* — *-the* — *-this* — *-possible*

19 *we hope* — *-that* — *-this* — *-it*

20 *of course* — *-it is* — *-it will*

21 *be done* — *can-* — *should-* — *could-*

SPELLING REVIEW

Transcribe the following words in longhand. All of them appear in the margins of the Reading and Writing Practice of this lesson.

1 .... 5 ....

2 .... 6 ....

3 .... 7 ....

4 .... 8 ....

BUSINESS VOCABULARY BUILDER

Write the underscored words in longhand; then define them briefly.

1 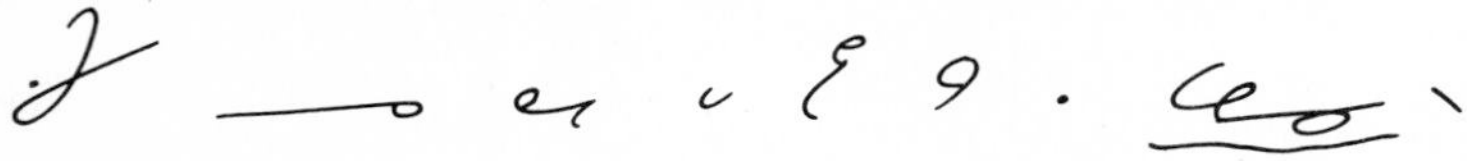

....

2 

....

3 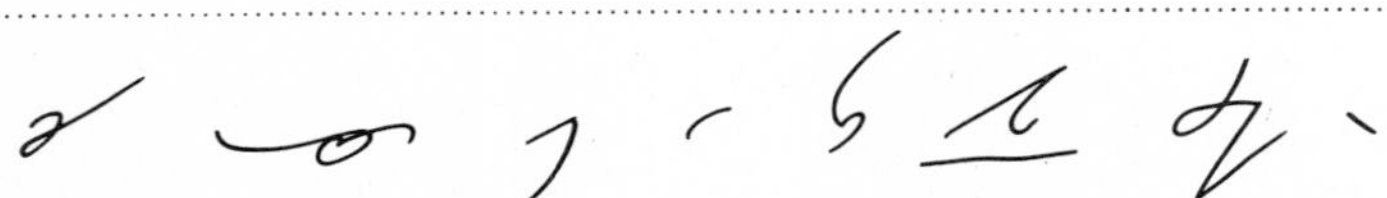

....

NAME ____________________ DATE ____________

Lesson 54

EVOLUTION DRILLS

In the spaces provided, write the correct shorthand forms.

1 *inform*  *-s* *-ed* *-ation*

2 *build*  *-s* *-ing* *-ings*

3 *entertain*  *-ing* *-ed* *-s*

4 *report*  *-s* *-ed* *-r*

5 *dismiss*  *-s* *-ing* *-ed*

SIMILAR-WORDS DRILL

In the following sentences, transcribe the underscored words.

1  ....

2 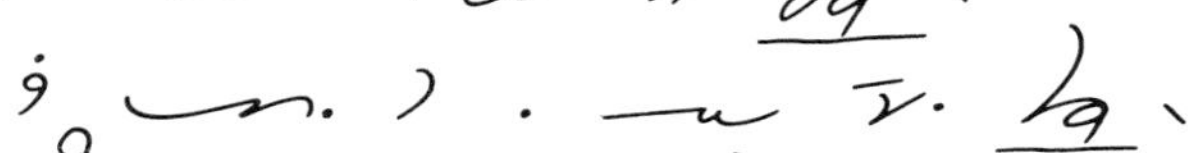 ....

3 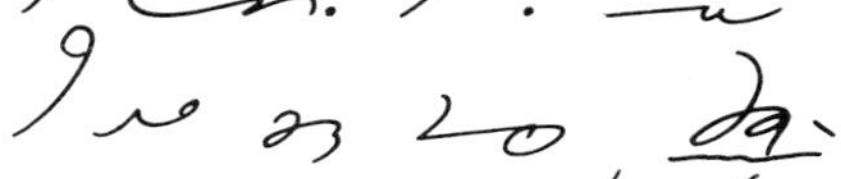 ....

4  ....

BUSINESS VOCABULARY BUILDER

Write the underscored words in longhand; then define them briefly.

1 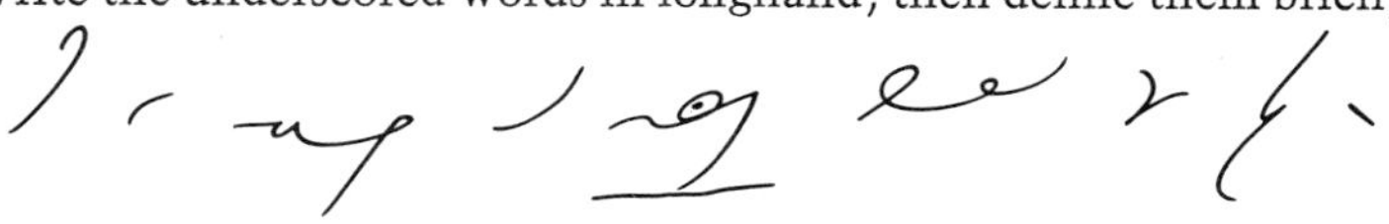

....

2 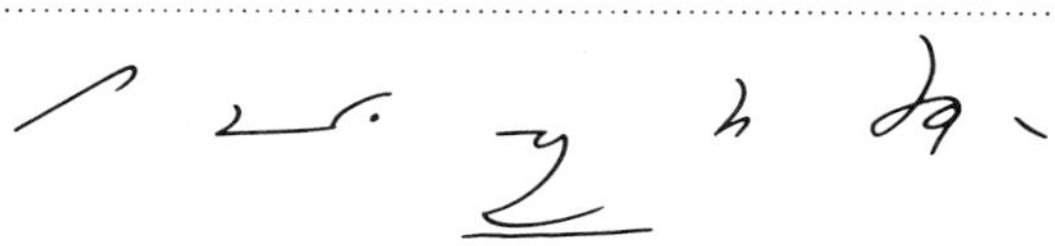

....

3 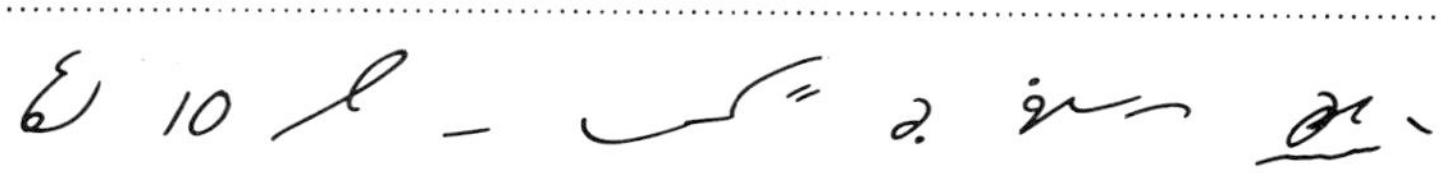

....

PUNCTUATION AND SPELLING

Punctuate the following sentences and write in longhand the spelling words indicated. Follow the directions on page 69.

Reason for Punctuation

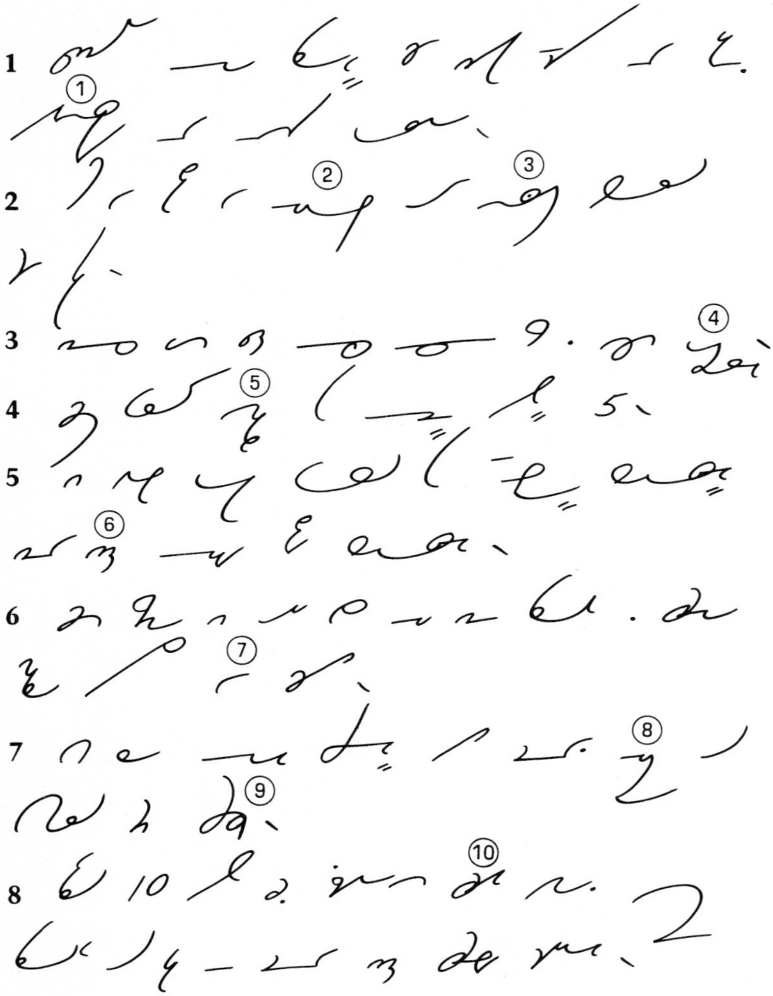

Spelling Words

1 .... 6 ....

2 .... 7 ....

3 .... 8 ....

4 .... 9 ....

5 .... 10 ....

NAME____ DATE____________________

Lesson 55

EVOLUTION DRILLS

In the spaces provided, write the correct shorthand forms.

1 *convince*  *-s* *-ing* *-ingly*

2 *improve*  *-s* *-d* *-ment*

3 *part*  *-ner* *-nership* *-nerships*

4 *locality*  *-s* *majority*  *-s*

5 *circulate*  *-s* *-ing* *-d*

GRAMMAR CHECKUP

The following sentences contain split infinitives. Indicate, as in the example below, where the word "splitting" the infinitive should be transferred to make the sentence read smoothly.

Example: 

1 

2 

3 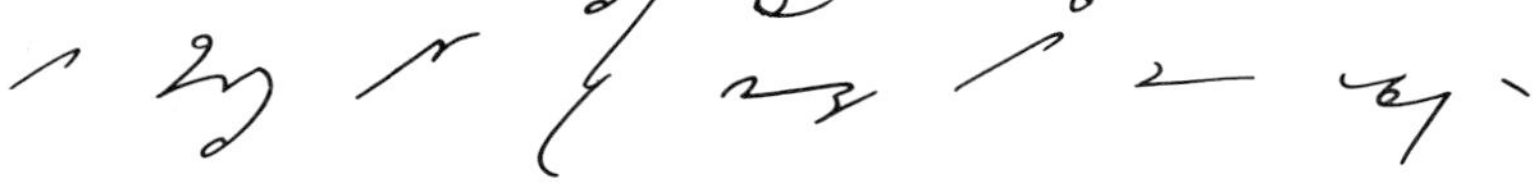

BUSINESS VOCABULARY BUILDER

Write the underscored words in longhand; then define them briefly.

1 

....

2 

....

PUNCTUATION AND SPELLING

Punctuate the following sentences and write in longhand the spelling words indicated. Follow the directions on page 69.

Reason for Punctuation

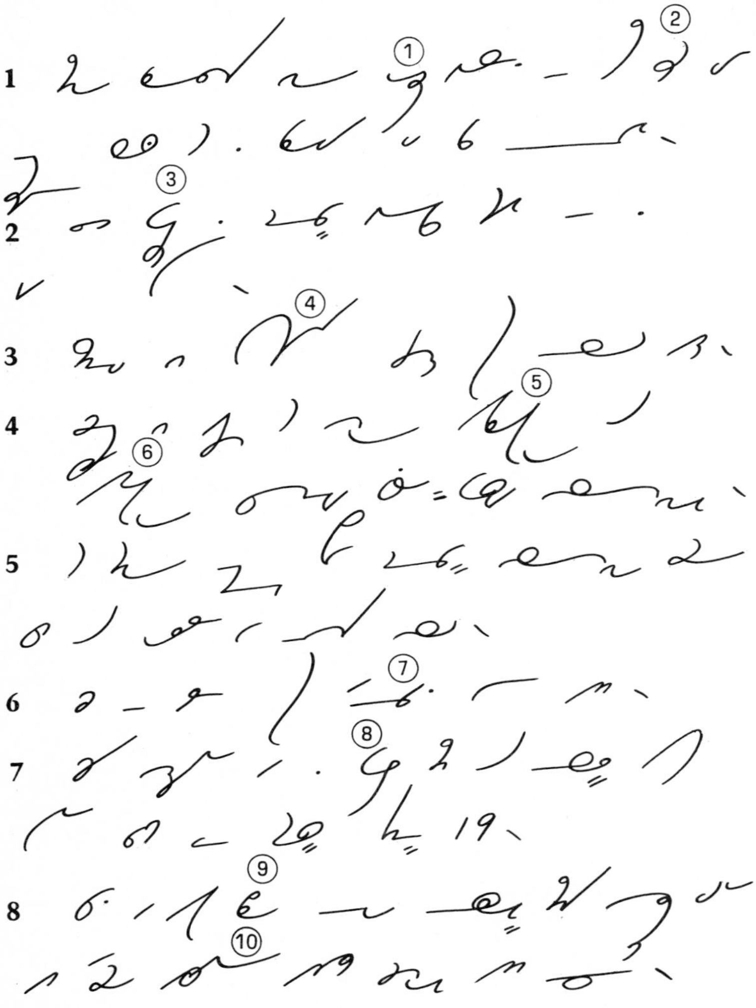

Spelling Words

1 .... 6 ....

2 .... 7 ....

3 .... 8 ....

4 .... 9 ....

5 .... 10 ....

NAME ______________________________ DATE ______________

Lesson 56

EVOLUTION DRILLS

In the spaces provided, write the correct shorthand forms.

1 *mistake*   *-s*   *-n*   *-nly*

2 *supervise*   *-ing*   *-r*   *-d*

3 *self-made*   *-defense*   *-control*   *-confidence*

4 *neighborhood*   *parent-*   *child-*   *likeli-*

5 *consult*   *-s*   *-ed*   *-ation*

6 *cablegram*   *dia-*   *pro-*   *tele-*

7 *electric*   *-wire*   *-motor*   *-car*

COMMON PREFIXES

Super- means ....

Define the following words briefly:

1 *supervisor* ....

2 *superior* ....

3 *superfluous* ....

BUSINESS VOCABULARY BUILDER

Write the underscored words in longhand; then define them briefly.

1 

....

2 

....

PUNCTUATION AND SPELLING

Punctuate the following sentences and write in longhand the spelling words indicated. Follow the directions on page 69.

Reason for Punctuation

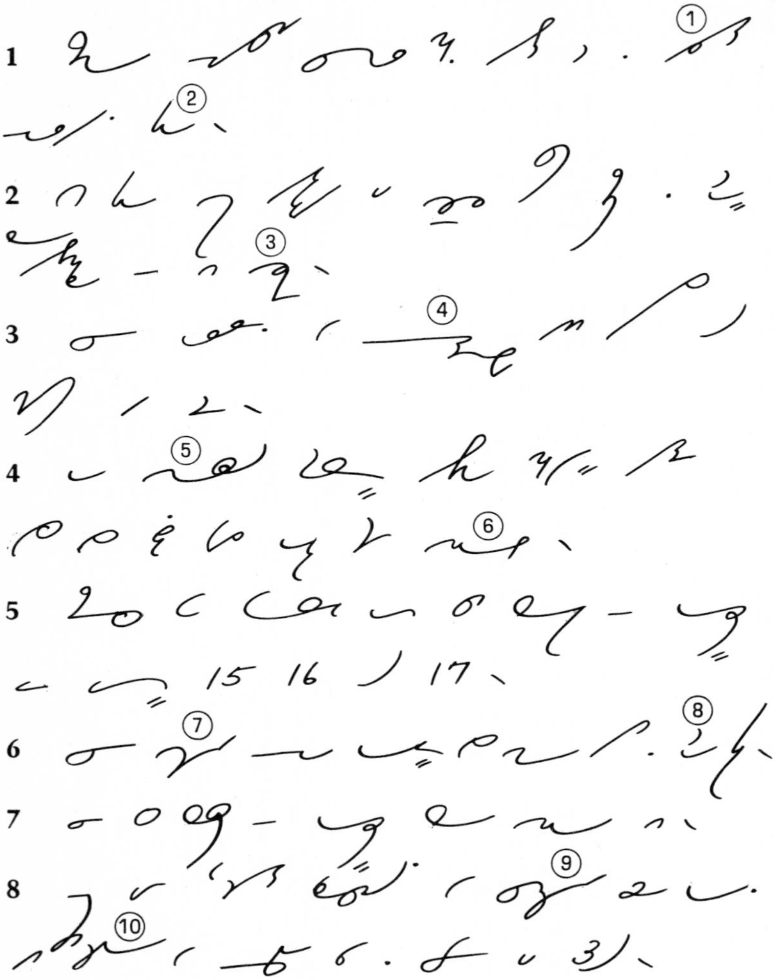

Spelling Words

1 .... 6 ....

2 .... 7 ....

3 .... 8 ....

4 .... 9 ....

5 .... 10 ....

NAME____ DATE____________________

Lesson 57

EVOLUTION DRILLS

In the spaces provided, write the correct shorthand forms.

1 *suggest*  -s -ed -tion

2 *govern*  -s -r -ment

3 *advertise*  -ing -d -ment

4 *manufacture*  -d -r -rs

5 *progress*  -ed -s -ive

6 *advantage*  -s -ous -ously

7 *recognize*  -d -ing -s

SPELLING FAMILIES

Add either *-able* or *-ible* to the following word beginnings to obtain the correct spelling of each word.

avail........................ *profit*........................ *comfort*........................

sens........................ *desir*........................ *valu*........................

suit........................ *poss*........................ *reason*........................

BUSINESS VOCABULARY BUILDER

Write the underscored words in longhand; then define them briefly.

1 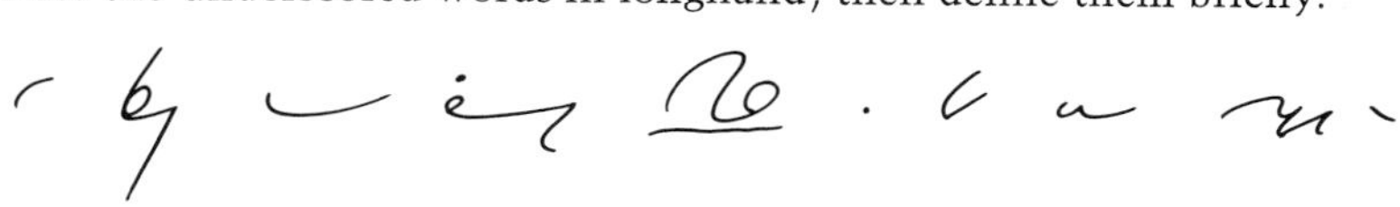

....

2 

....

3 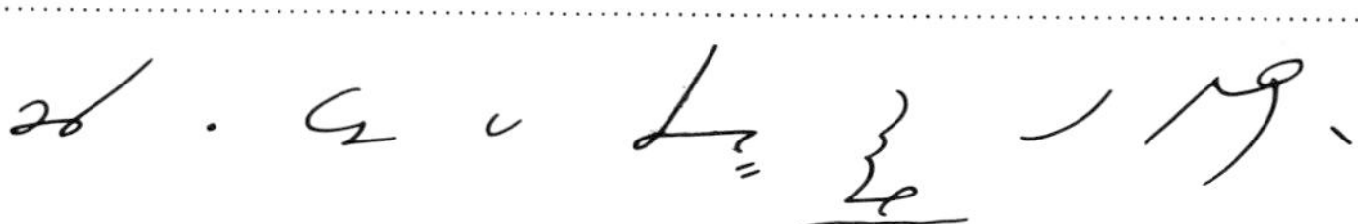

....

PUNCTUATION AND SPELLING

Punctuate the following sentences and write in longhand the spelling words indicated. Follow the directions on page 69.

Reason for Punctuation

1 2 3 4 5 6 7 8

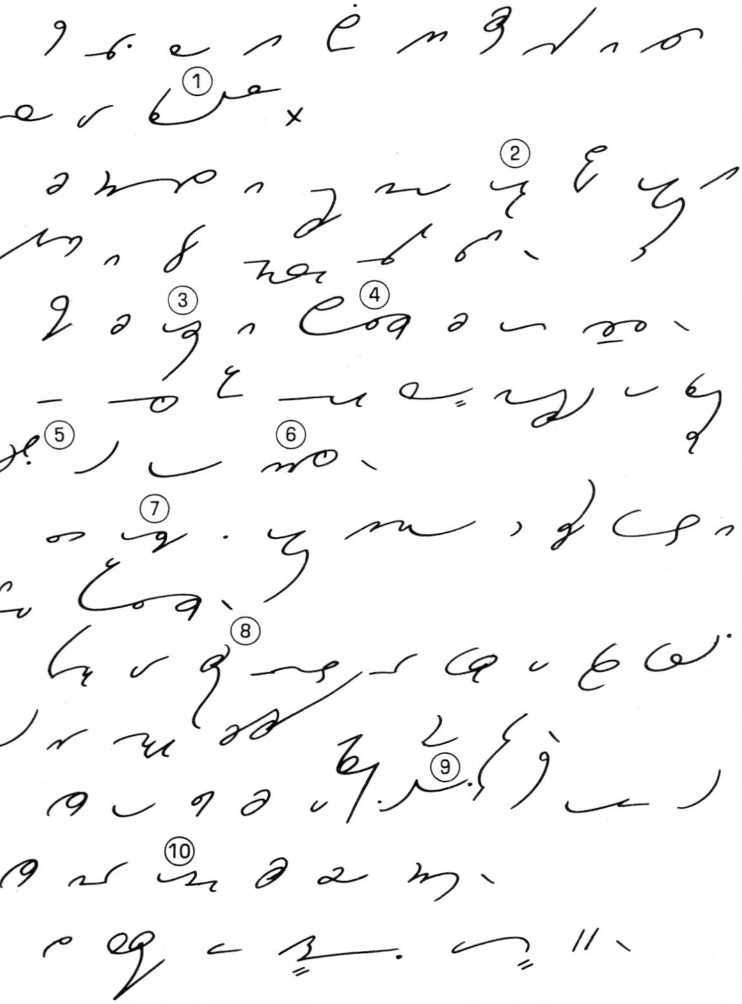

Spelling Words

1

2

3

4

5

6

7

8

9

10

NAME____DATE____________________

Lesson 58

EVOLUTION DRILLS

In the spaces provided, write the correct shorthand forms.

1 *days ago*   *weeks-*   *years-*   *months-*

2 *I wanted*   *he-*   *we-*   *who-*

3 *some of these*   *-them*   *-that*   *-the*

4 *let us*   *-know*   *-have*   *-see*

5 *to be*   *-have*   *-place*   *-perform*

6 *thank you for*   *-the*   *-this*   *-your order*

GRAMMAR CHECKUP

Underscore the word or expression that is not in parallel construction in the following sentences. Indicate in the space provided the expression you would use to make it parallel.

Example:

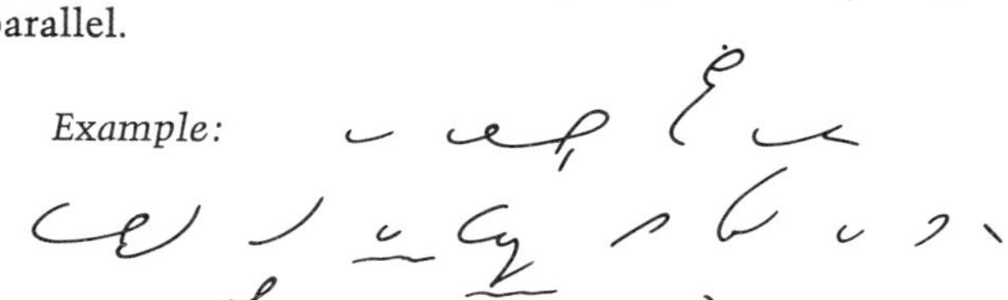

profitable

1

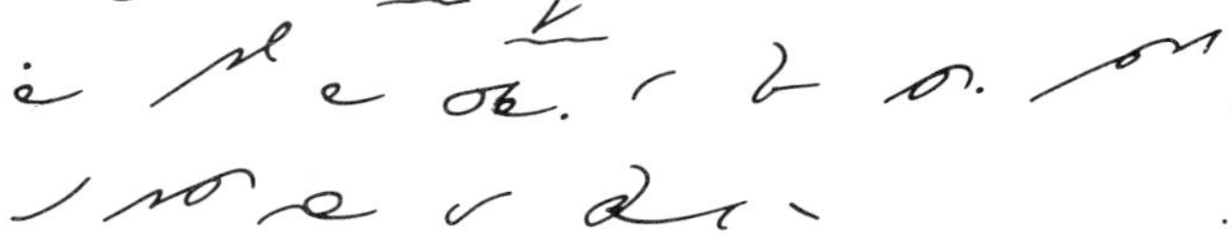

....

....

2

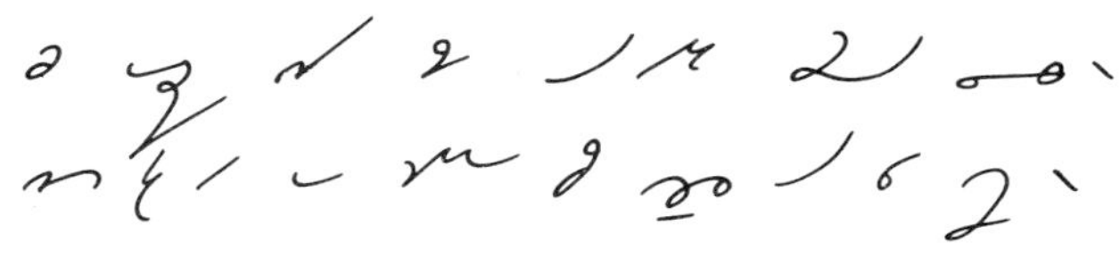

....

3 ....

BUSINESS VOCABULARY BUILDER

Write the underscored words in longhand; then define them briefly.

1

....

2

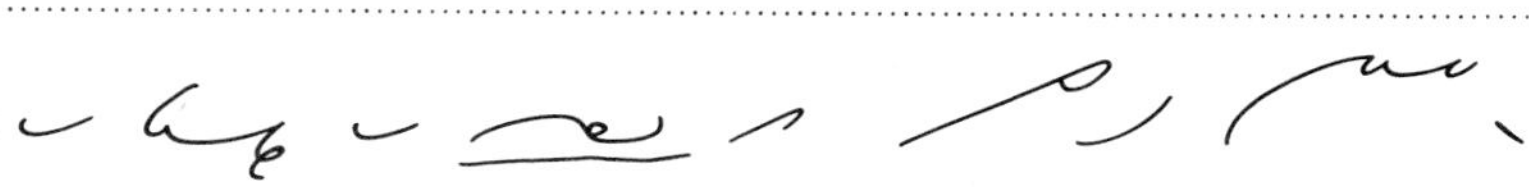

....

PUNCTUATION AND SPELLING

Punctuate the following sentences and write in longhand the spelling words indicated. Follow the directions on page 69.

Reason for Punctuation

Spelling Words

1 .... 6 ....

2 .... 7 ....

3 .... 8 ....

4 .... 9 ....

5 .... 10 ....

NAME________________________________ DATE________________

Lesson 59

EVOLUTION DRILLS

In the spaces provided, write the correct shorthand forms.

1 *deserve*  *-s* *-ing* *-d*

2 *explain*  *-s* *-ed* *-ation*

3 *become*  *-s* *-ing* *-ingly*

4 *replace*  *-s* *-d* *-ment*

5 *enforce*  *-s* *-d* *-ment*

6 *misplace*  *-d* *-s* *-ment*

SPELLING FAMILIES

Add either *-cial* or *-tial* to the following word beginnings to complete each word correctly.

commer........ *poten*........ *benefi*........

finan........ *substan*........ *spe*........

par........ *offi*........ *so*........

BUSINESS VOCABULARY BUILDER

Write the underscored words in longhand; then define them briefly.

1 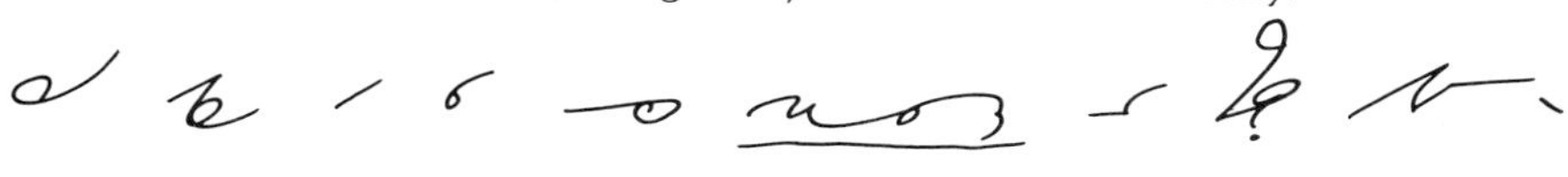

....

2 

....

3 

....

PUNCTUATION AND SPELLING

Punctuate the following sentences and write in longhand the spelling words indicated. Follow the directions on page 69.

Reason for Punctuation

Spelling Words

1 ....

2 ....

3 ....

4 ....

5 ....

6 ....

7 ....

8 ....

9 ....

10 ....

NAME ______________________ DATE ______________

Lesson 60

EVOLUTION DRILLS

In the spaces provided, write the correct shorthand forms.

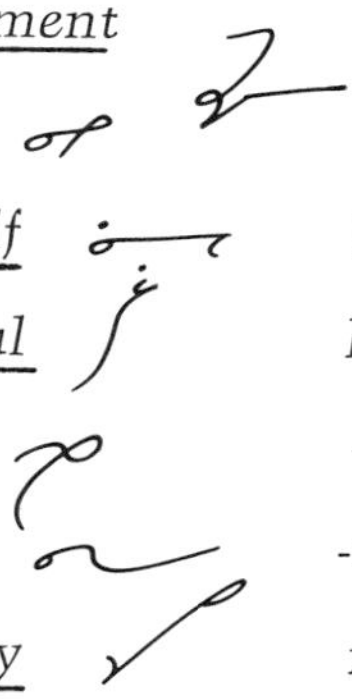

1	*investment*	*adjust-*	*require-*	*amuse-*
2	*initial*	*-s*	*-ing*	*-ed*
3	*himself*	*her-*	*my-*	*your-*
4	*hopeful*	*help-*	*doubt-*	*fear-*
5	*cable*	*-s*	*-ing*	*-d*
6	*equal*	*-ize*	*-izer*	*-ly*
7	*steadily*	*read-*	*merr-*	*hast-*

COMMON PREFIXES

Re- means ....

Define the following words briefly:

1 *replenish* ....

2 *repeat* ....

3 *reconsider* ....

4 *reconfirm* ....

BUSINESS VOCABULARY BUILDER

Write the underscored words in longhand; then define them briefly.

1 

....

2 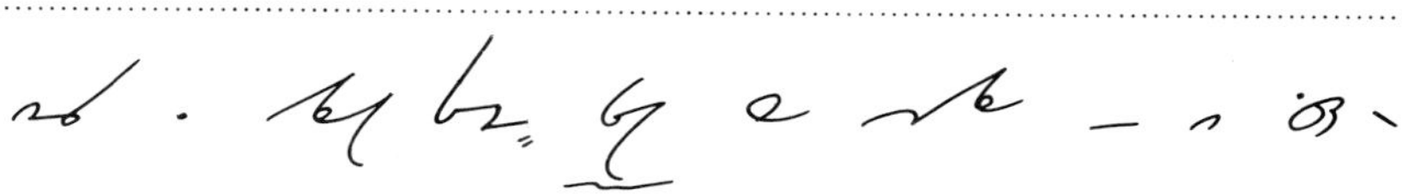

....

3 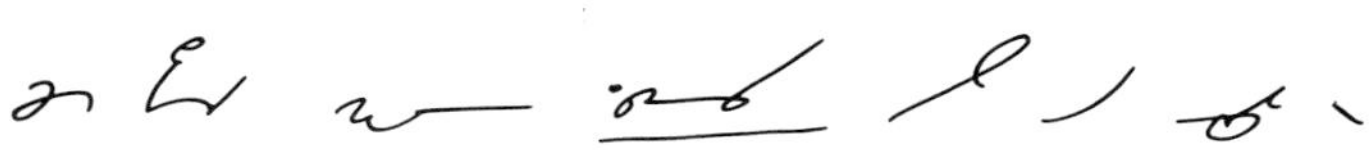

....

PUNCTUATION AND SPELLING

Punctuate the following sentences and write in longhand the spelling words indicated. Follow the directions on page 69.

Reason for Punctuation

Spelling Words

1 ....
2 ....
3 ....
4 ....
5 ....
6 ....
7 ....
8 ....
9 ....
10 ....

NAME______________________________ DATE______________

Lesson 61

EVOLUTION DRILLS

In the spaces provided, write the correct shorthand forms.

1 electric razor  -toaster -light -fan

2 entertain  -s -ing -ed

3 transport  -s -ed -ation

4 self-reliant   -assurance -confidence -determination

5 interest  -ed -ing -ingly

6 circumstance  -s circumstantial  -ly

7 supervise  -ing -d -r

8 overcome  -paid -turn -power

SPELLING REVIEW

Transcribe the following words in longhand. All of them appear in the Reading and Writing Practice of Lesson 61.

1  ....

2  ....

3  ....

4  ....

5  ....

6  ....

7  ....

8  ....

BUSINESS VOCABULARY BUILDER

Write the underscored words in longhand; then define them briefly.

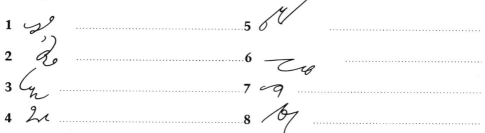

1 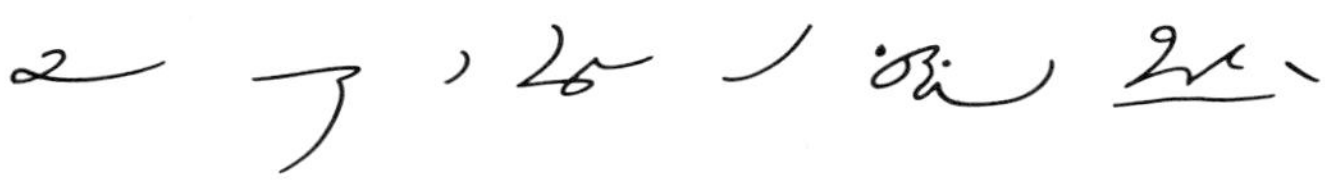

....

2 

....

3 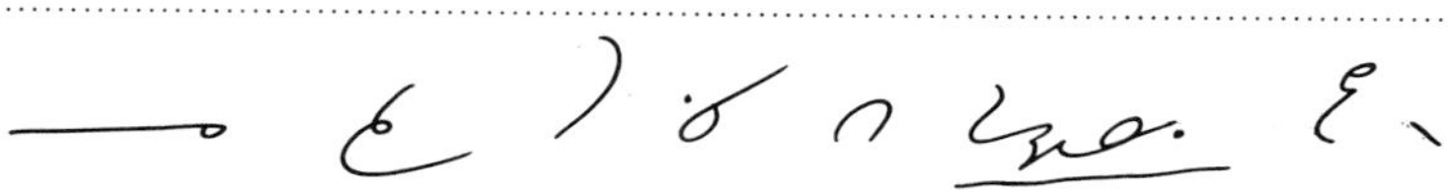

....

PUNCTUATION AND SPELLING

Punctuate the following sentences and write in longhand the spelling words indicated. Follow the directions on page 69.

Reason for Punctuation

Spelling Words

1	6 ......
2	7 ......
3	8 ......
4	9 ......
5	10 ......

NAME____DATE____________________

Lesson 62

EVOLUTION DRILLS

In the spaces provided, write the correct shorthand forms.

1 *tabulate*  *-ing* *-r* *-d*

2 *reward*  *-s* *-ing* *-ed*

3 *sparingly*  *will-* *know-* *grudg-*

4 *minority*  *-s* *facility*  *-s*

5 *upward*  *in-* *out-* *back-*

6 *monogram*  *pro-* *cable-* *radio-*

7 *neighborhood*  *parent-* *child-* *woman-*

SIMILAR-WORDS DRILL

Transcribe the underscored expression in the space provided.

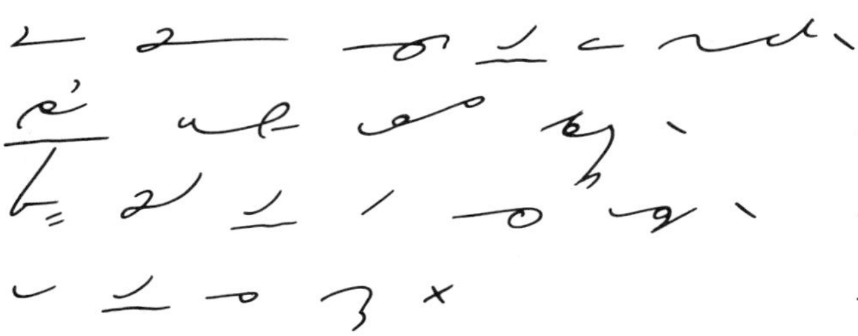

1 ....

2 ....

3 ....

4 ....

BUSINESS VOCABULARY BUILDER

Write the underscored words in longhand; then define them briefly.

1 

....

2 

....

PUNCTUATION AND SPELLING

Punctuate the following sentences and write in longhand the spelling words indicated. Follow the directions on page 69.

Reason for Punctuation

Spelling Words

1 .... 6 ....

2 .... 7 ....

3 .... 8 ....

4 .... 9 ....

5 .... 10 ....

NAME ______________________ DATE ______________

Lesson 63

EVOLUTION DRILLS

In the spaces provided, write the correct shorthand forms.

1 *direct* 	*-s*	*-r*	*-rs*
2 *unfold* 	*-s*	*-ing*	*-ed*
3 *comply* 	*-s*	*-d*	*-ance*
4 *increase* 	*-s*	*-ing*	*-ingly*
5 *extend* 	*-s*	*-ing*	*-ed*
6 *below* 	*-long*	*-come*	*-came*
7 *replenish* 	*-s*	*-ing*	*-ed*

COMMON PREFIXES

Un- means ....

1 *unusual* ....

2 *uncertain* ....

3 *unquestioned* ....

4 *unprecedented* ....

5 *unnecessary* ....

BUSINESS VOCABULARY BUILDER

Write the underscored words in longhand; then define them briefly.

1 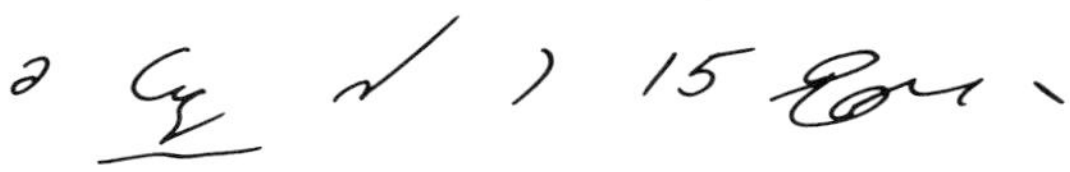

....

2 

....

PUNCTUATION AND SPELLING

Punctuate the following sentences and write in longhand the spelling words indicated. Follow the directions on page 69.

Reason for Punctuation

Spelling Words

1 .... 6 ....

2 .... 7 ....

3 .... 8 ....

4 .... 9 ....

5 .... 10 ....

NAME ______________________ DATE ______________

Lesson 64

EVOLUTION DRILLS

In the spaces provided, write the correct shorthand forms.

1 *smudge*  -s -ing -d

2 *addition*  -s -al -ally

3 *serious*  -ly -ness

4 *reader*  lead- near- dear-

5 *judge*  -s -ing -ment

6 *secure*  -s -ing -d

7 *schedule*  -s -ing -d

SPELLING FAMILIES

Transcribe the following words. Some end in *-er;* others in *-or;* still others in *-ar.*

1  ....

2  ....

3  ....

4  ....

5  ....

6 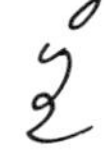 ....

7  ....

8  ....

BUSINESS VOCABULARY BUILDER

Write the underscored words in longhand; then define them briefly.

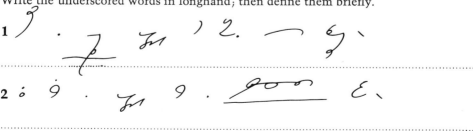

1 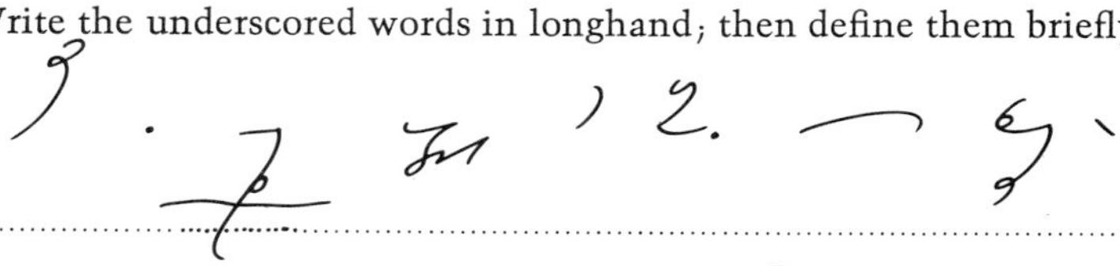

....

2 

....

3 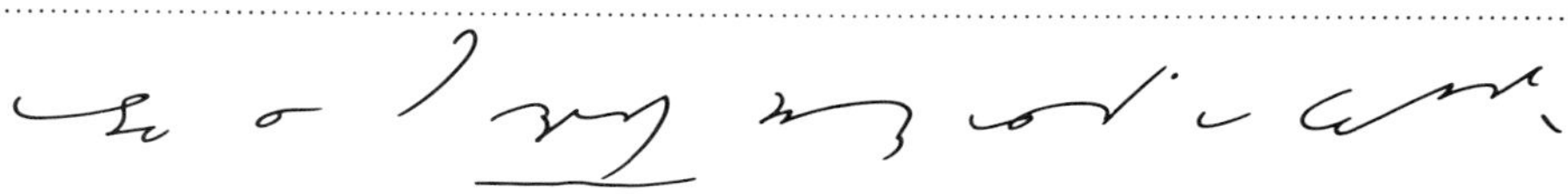

....

PUNCTUATION AND SPELLING

Punctuate the following sentences and write in longhand the spelling words indicated. Follow the directions on page 69.

Reason for Punctuation

Spelling Words

1 .... 6 ....

2 .... 7 ....

3 .... 8 ....

4 .... 9 ....

5 .... 10 ....

NAME______________________________ DATE______________

Lesson 65

EVOLUTION DRILLS

In the spaces provided, write the correct shorthand forms.

1 *land* -ed -ing -ings

2 *tender* -s -ed -ly

3 *friend* -ly -liness -ship

4 *differ* -ing -ence -ent

5 *contemplate* -s -ing -d

6 *examine* -s -ing -ation

7 *determine* -s -ing -ation

SIMILAR-WORDS DRILL

Within the parentheses in each of the following sentences write in longhand either *brought* or *bought*—whichever is correct.

1
2
3
4

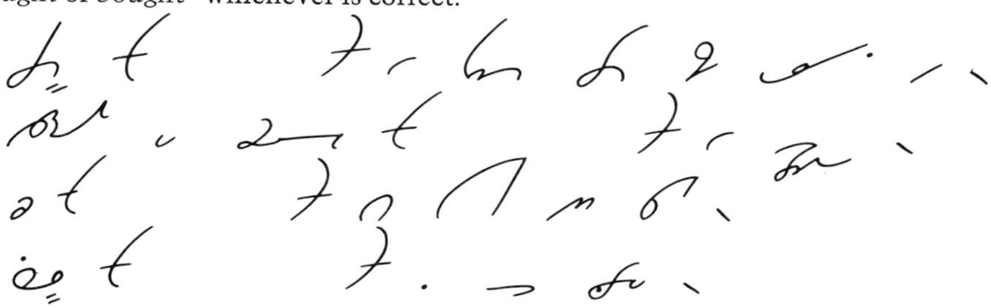

BUSINESS VOCABULARY BUILDER

Write the underscored words in longhand; then define them briefly.

1

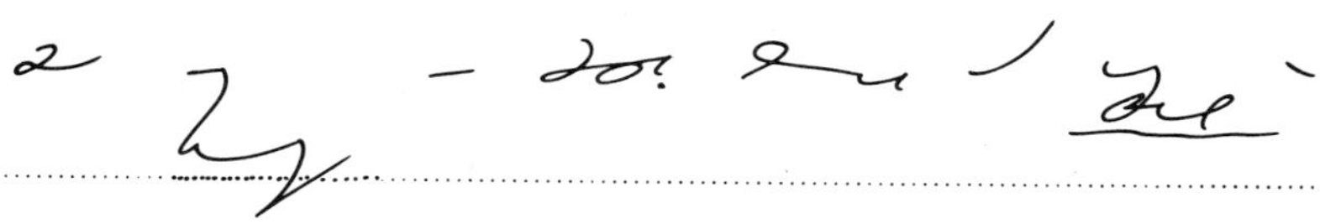

2

3

PUNCTUATION AND SPELLING

Punctuate the following sentences and write in longhand the spelling words indicated. Follow the directions on page 69.

Reason for Punctuation

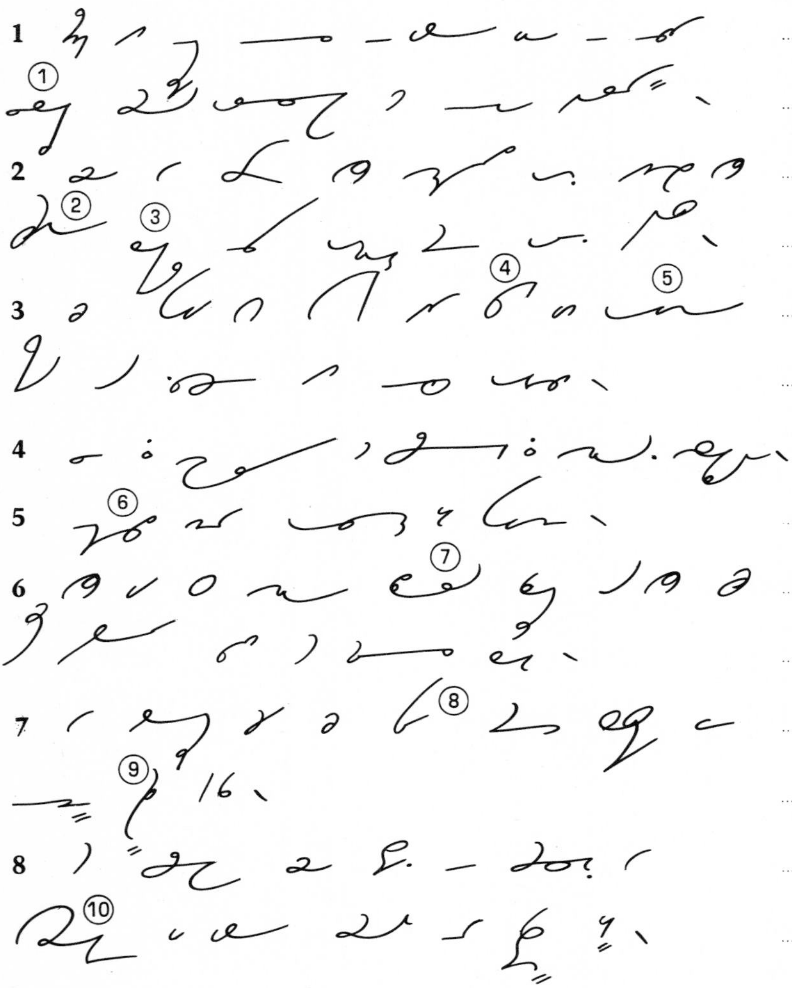

Spelling Words

1. ....
2. ....
3. ....
4. ....
5. ....
6. ....
7. ....
8. ....
9. ....
10. ....

NAME ______________________________ DATE ______________

Lesson 66

EVOLUTION DRILLS

In the spaces provided, write the correct shorthand forms.

1 *acknowledge*   -s   -d   -ment

2 *any*   -one   -where   -how

3 *short*   -ly   -r   -n

4 *experience*   -s   -ing   -d

5 *wish*   -s   -ing   -ful

6 *question*   -s   -ed   -ble

7 *something*   any-   every-   no-

COMMON PREFIXES

Pro- means ....

Define the following words briefly:

1 *proceed* ....

2 *progress* ....

3 *procedure* ....

4 *promotion* ....

BUSINESS VOCABULARY BUILDER

Write the underscored words in longhand; then define them briefly.

1 

....

2 

....

PUNCTUATION AND SPELLING

Punctuate the following sentences and write in longhand the spelling words indicated. Follow the directions on page 69.

Reason for Punctuation

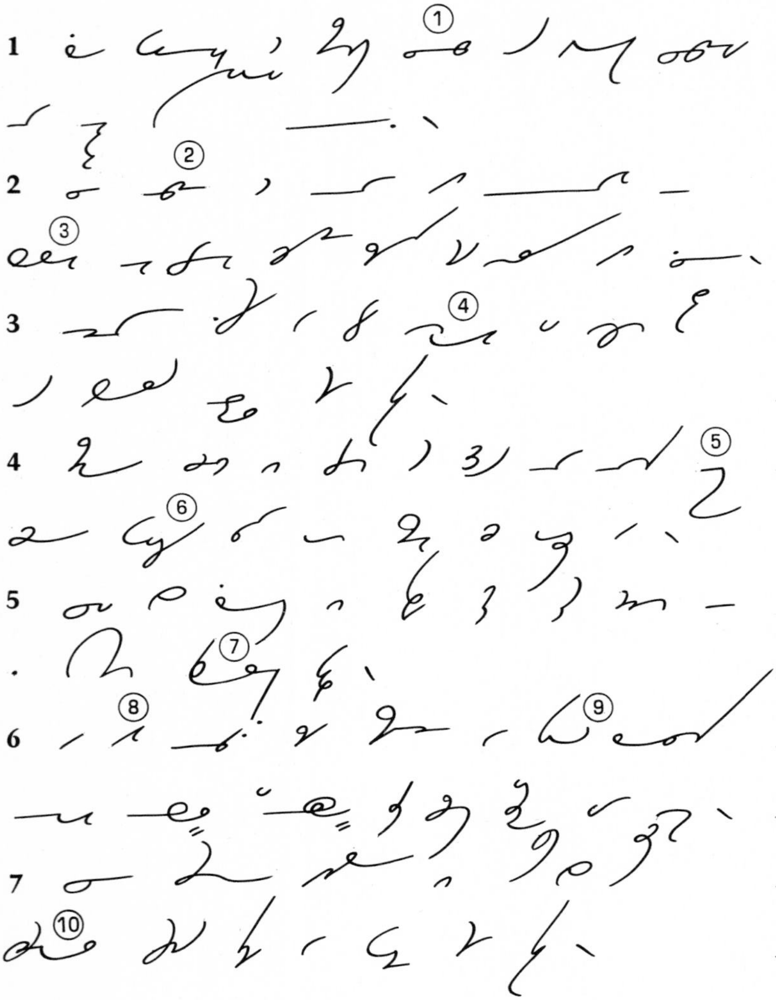

Spelling Words

1 .... 6 ....

2 .... 7 ....

3 .... 8 ....

4 .... 9 ....

5 .... 10 ....

NAME______________________________ DATE______________

Lesson 67

EVOLUTION DRILLS

In the spaces provided, write the correct shorthand forms.

1 *I hope you*  *-can* *-will* *-are*

2 *we hope you*  *-can* *-will* *-are*

3 *have been able*  *I-* *you-* *we-*

4 *one of them*  *-the* *-our* *-these*

5 *to me*  *-make* *-know*

6 *to be*  *-have* *-fly* *-blame*

GRAMMAR CHECKUP

One of the words in parentheses is correct. Underscore that word and transcribe it in longhand in the space provided.

1 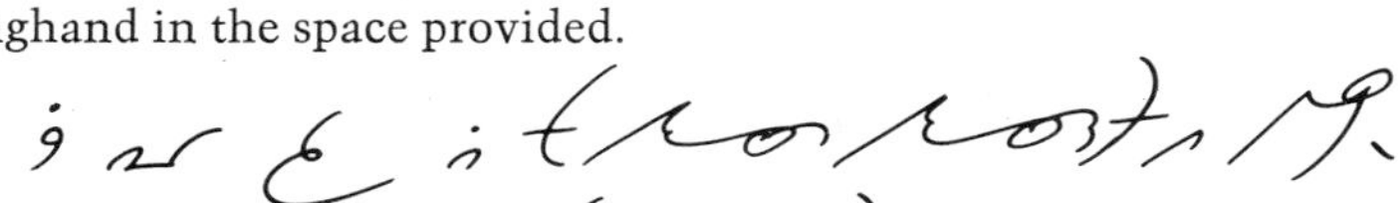 ....

2  ....

3  ....

....

4  ....

BUSINESS VOCABULARY BUILDER

Write the underscored words in longhand; then define them briefly.

1 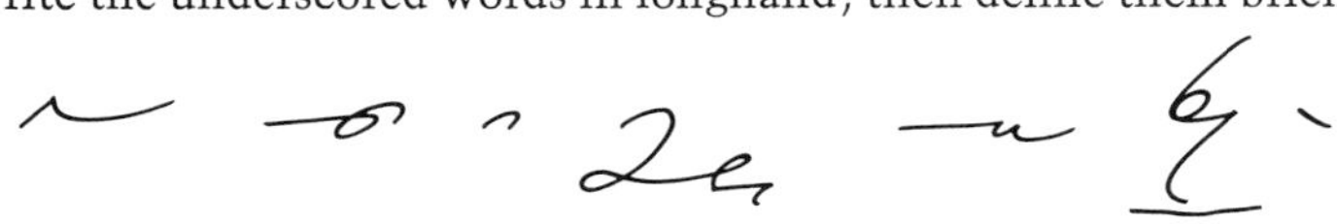

....

2 

....

PUNCTUATION AND SPELLING

Punctuate the following sentences and write in longhand the spelling words indicated. Follow the directions on page 69.

Reason for Punctuation

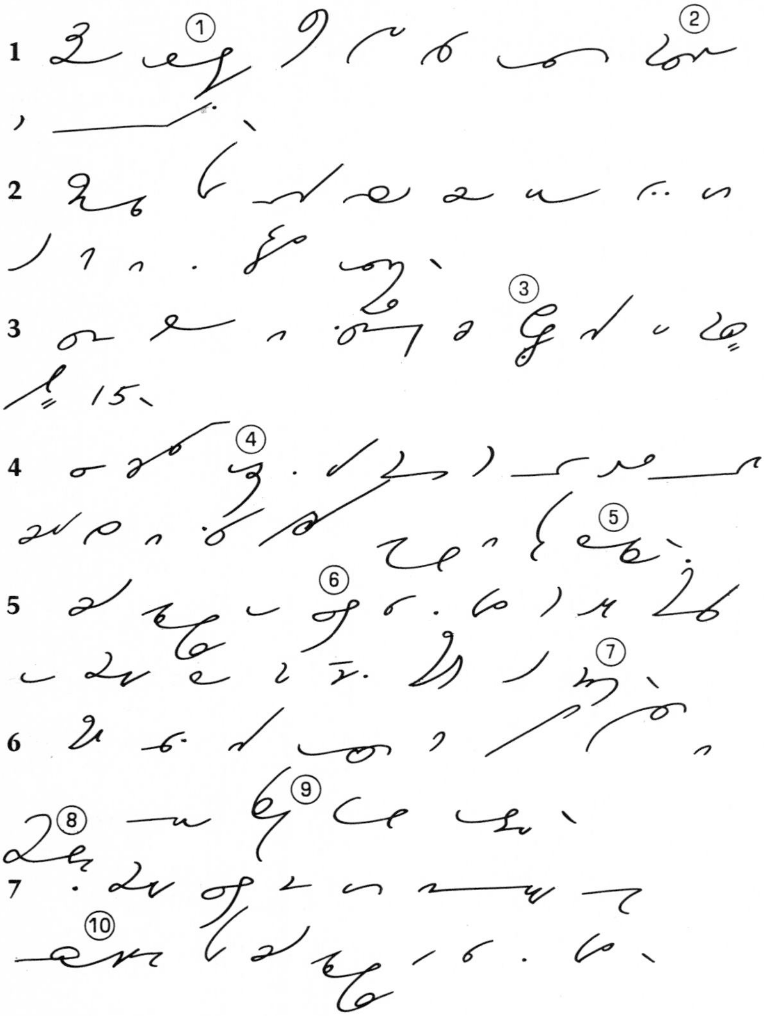

Spelling Words

1 ....

2 ....

3 ....

4 ....

5 ....

6 ....

7 ....

8 ....

9 ....

10 ....

NAME________________________________ DATE______________

Lesson 68

EVOLUTION DRILLS

In the spaces provided, write the correct shorthand forms.

1 *require* | -s | -d | -ment

2 *photograph* | -s | -ed | -r

3 *contribute* | -s | -d | -r

4 *frequent* | -ly | *infrequent* | -ly

5 *attitude* | -s | *aptitude* | -s

6 *substitution* | in- | con-

7 *privilege* | -s | -d

SIMILAR-WORDS DRILL

Transcribe the underscored words in the space provided.

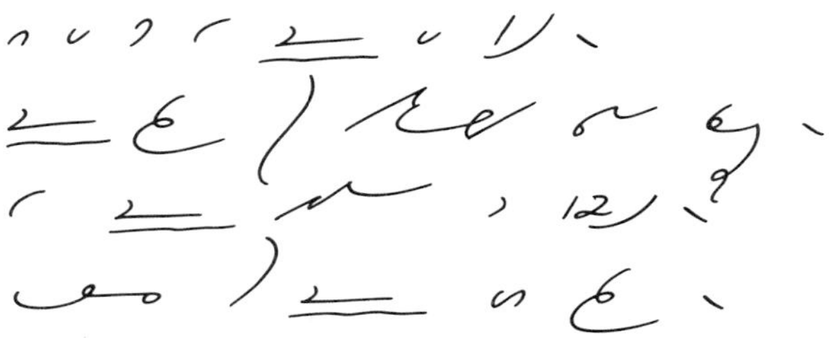

1 ....

2 ....

3 ....

4 ....

BUSINESS VOCABULARY BUILDER

Write the underscored words in longhand; then define them briefly.

1 

....

2 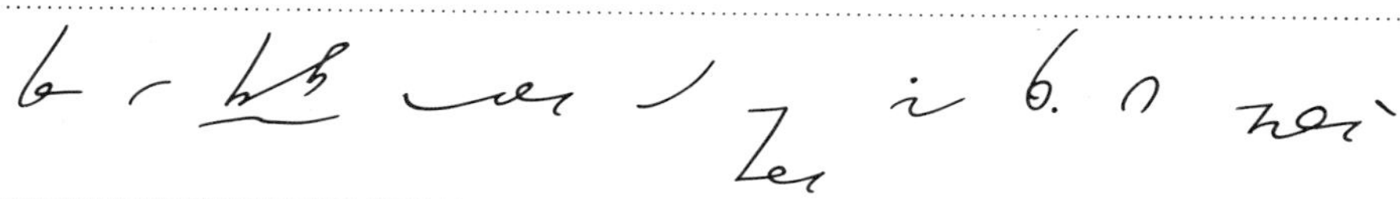

....

3 

....

PUNCTUATION AND SPELLING

Punctuate the following sentences and write in longhand the spelling words indicated. Follow the directions on page 69.

Reason for Punctuation

Spelling Words

1 ____________ 6 ____________

2 ____________ 7 ____________

3 ____________ 8 ____________

4 ____________ 9 ____________

5 ____________ 10 ____________

NAME____ DATE______________________

Lesson 69

EVOLUTION DRILLS

In the spaces provided, write the correct shorthand forms.

1 *element*  *-s* *-al* *-ary*

2 *ourselves*  *them-* *your-*

3 *efficient*  *-ly* *proficient*  *-ly*

4 *trouble*  *-s* *-d* *-ing*

5 *station*  *-s* *-ing* *-ed*

6 *substantial*  *-ly* *credential*  *-s*

7 *equal*  *-s* *-ize* *-ing*

COMMON PREFIXES

Pre- means ....

1 *predict* ....

2 *preliminary* ....

3 *premature* ....

4 *presume* ....

BUSINESS VOCABULARY BUILDER

Write the underscored words in longhand; then define them briefly.

1 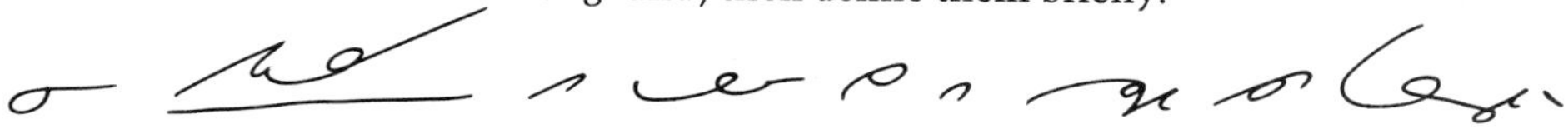

....

2 . 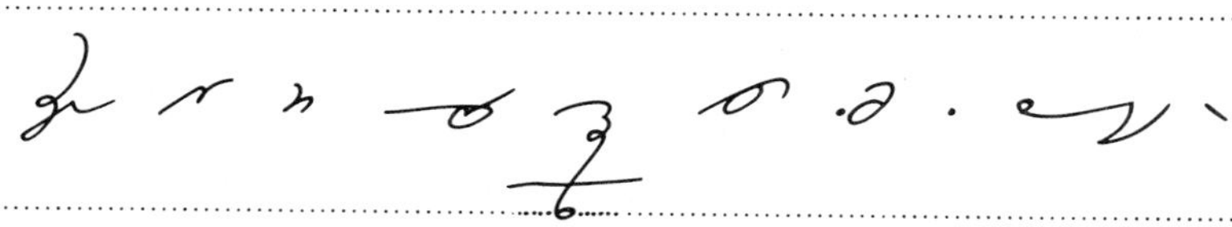

....

3 

....

PUNCTUATION AND SPELLING

Punctuate the following sentences and write in longhand the spelling words indicated. Follow the directions on page 69.

Reason for Punctuation

Spelling Words

1 .... 6 ....

2 .... 7 ....

3 .... 8 ....

4 .... 9 ....

5 .... 10 ....

NAME________________________________ DATE ______________

Lesson 70

EVOLUTION DRILLS

In the spaces provided, write the correct shorthand forms.

1 *contain*  -s -ing -r

2 *employ*  -s -ed -ment

3 *reform*  -s -ed -ation

4 *discourage*  -d -ing -ment

5 *confer*  -s -ed -ence

6 *connect*  -s -ed -ing

7 *invest*  -r -rs -ment

SPELLING FAMILIES

Add *ize, ise,* or *yze* to the following word beginnings to complete each word correctly.

apolog.................... *anal*.................... *enterpr*....................

compr.................... *recogn*.................... *util*....................

real.................... *organ*.................... *paral*....................

BUSINESS VOCABULARY BUILDER

Write the underscored words in longhand; then define them briefly.

1 

....

2 

....

3 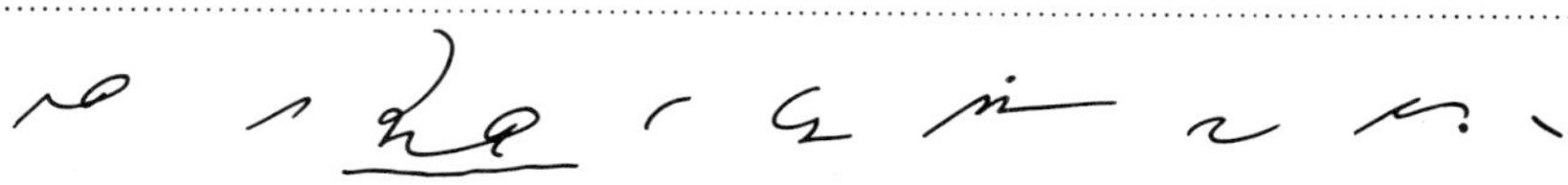

....

PUNCTUATION AND SPELLING

Punctuate the following sentences and write in longhand the spelling words indicated. Follow the directions on page 69.

Reason for Punctuation

1 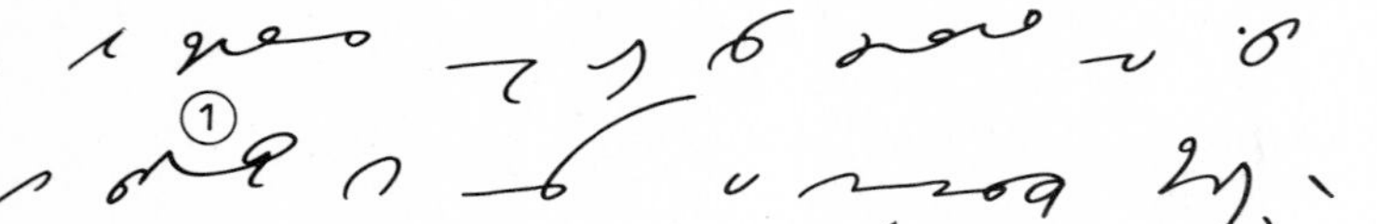

2 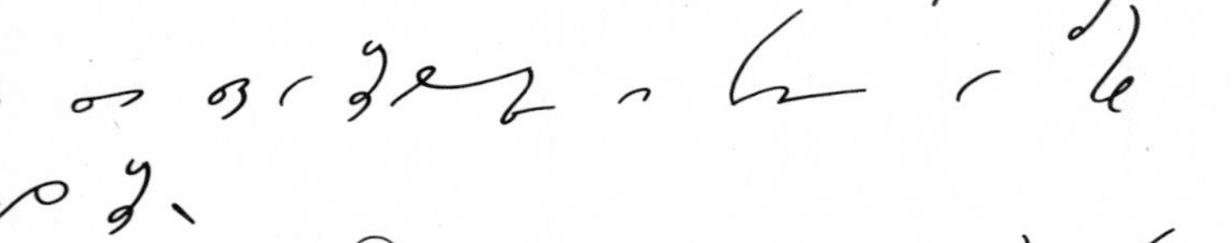

3 

4 

5 

6 

7 

Spelling Words

1 .... 6 ....

2 .... 7 ....

3 .... 8 ....

4 .... 9 ....

5 .... 10 ....

Appendix: Summary of Punctuation Rules

Summary of punctuation rules

, parenthetical

A word or phrase that is used parenthetically (that is, one not necessary to the grammatical completeness of the sentence) should be set off by commas.

If the parenthetical expression occurs at the end of the sentence, only one comma is used.

There is, of course, *no charge for our services.*

Please let us know, Mr. Strong, *if we can help you.*

We actually print your picture on the card, Ms. Green.

, apposition

An expression in apposition (that is, a word or a phrase or a clause that identifies or explains other terms) should be set off by commas. When an expression in apposition occurs at the end of a sentence, only one comma is necessary.

My employer, Mr. Frank Smith, *is on a business trip.*

I will see him on Friday, June 15, *at 3 o'clock.*

His book, Principles of Accounting, *is out of stock.*

For more information call Mr. Brown, our production manager.

▶ Note: When the clarifying term is very closely connected with the principal noun so that the sense would not be complete without the added term, no commas are required.

My brother Fred *arrived yesterday.*

The word embarrassed *is often misspelled.*

, series

When the last member of a series of three or more items is preceded by *and* or *or,* place a comma before the conjunction as well as between the other items.

For his birthday he received a tie, a shirt, and a wallet.

I need a person to take dictation, to answer the phone, and to greet callers.

I can see her on July 18, on July 19, or on July 30.

▶ Note: Some authorities prefer to omit the comma before the conjunction. In your shorthand textbooks, however, the comma will always be inserted before the conjunction.

, if clause

A subordinate (or introductory) clause followed by a main clause is separated from the main clause by a comma. A subordinate clause is often introduced by subordinating conjunctions including *if, as, when, though, although, because,* and others. Subordinate clauses introduced by *if.*

If you complete the work before 5 o'clock, *you may leave.*

If I cannot come, *I will call you.*

If John is ill, *he should stay home.*

, as clause

A subordinate clause introduced by *as* and followed by a main clause is separated from the main clause by a comma.

As you know, *you have not yet paid your June bill.*

As I cannot attend the meeting, *I will send my assistant.*

, when clause

A clause introduced by *when* and followed by the main clause is separated from the main clause by a comma.

When I was in Dallas, *I attended three meetings.*

When you do not pay your bills, *you are endangering your credit.*

, introductory

A comma is used to separate a subordinate (or introductory) clause from a following main clause. You have already studied the application of this rule to subordinate clauses introduced by *if, as,* and *when.* Here are additional examples:

While I understand the statement, *I do not agree with it.*

Although it was only 3 o'clock, *he closed the office.*

Before you sign the contract, *discuss it with your lawyer.*

A comma is also used after introductory words or phrases such as *furthermore, on the contrary,* and *for instance.*

Furthermore, *the report was incomplete.*

On the contrary, *you are the one who is responsible.*

For your convenience in sending your check, *I am enclosing an envelope.*

Note: If the subordinate clause or other introductory expression follows the main clause, the comma is usually not necessary.

I am enclosing an envelope for your convenience in sending your check.

, conjunction

A comma is used to separate two independent clauses that are joined by one of these conjunctions: *and, but, or, for, nor.*

An independent clause (sometimes called a main or a principal clause) is one that has a subject and a predicate and that could stand alone as a complete sentence.

There are 15 people in my department, but *only 11 of them are here now.*

The first independent clause is:

There are 15 people in my department.

And the second independent clause is:

Only 11 of them are here now.

Both clauses could stand as separate sentences, with a period after each. Because the thoughts of the two clauses are closely related, however, the clauses were joined to form one sentence. Because the two independent clauses are connected by the conjunction *but,* a comma is used between them and is placed before the conjunction.

, and omitted

When two or more adjectives modify the same noun, they are separated by commas.

He was a quiet, efficient *worker.*

However, the comma is not used if the first adjective modifies the combined idea of the second adjective plus the noun.

The book was bound in an attractive brown *cloth.*

Note: You can quickly determine whether to insert a comma between two consecutive adjectives by mentally placing *and* between them. If the sentence makes good sense with *and* inserted between the adjectives, then the comma is used. For example, the first illustration would make good sense if it read:

He was a quiet and *efficient worker.*